WITHDRAWN
UTSA LIBRARIES

# WORDS AND SPACES

## An Anthology of
## Twentieth Century
## Musical Experiments
## in Language and
## Sonic Environments

**Stuart Saunders Smith**
**and**
**Thomas DeLio**
**Editors and Contributors**

UNIVERSITY
PRESS OF
AMERICA

Lanham • New York • London

Copyright © 1989 by

University Press of America,® Inc.

4720 Boston Way
Lanham, MD 20706

3 Henrietta Street
London WC2E 8LU England

All rights reserved

Printed in the United States of America

British Cataloging in Publication Information Available

## Library of Congress Cataloging-in-Publication Data

Words and spaces : an anthology of twentieth century musical experiments in language and
sonic environments / Stuart Saunders Smith and Thomas DeLio.
p.    cm.
1. Music—20th century—History and criticism.    2. Composition (Music)—20th century.
3. Music and language.    I. Smith, Stuart Saunders.    II. DeLio, Thomas, 1951–        .
ML197.W77      1989
780'.904—dc19        89–5609 CIP

ISBN 0–8191–7425–4 (alk. paper)
ISBN 0–8191–7426–2 (pbk.: alk. paper)

All University Press of America books are produced on acid-free paper.
The paper used in this publication meets the minimum requirements of American
National Standard for Information Sciences—Permanence of Paper for Printed Library
Materials, ANSI Z39.48–1984.      ∞

LIBRARY
The University of Texas
at San Antonio

To
Sylvia
and
Kathy

## Acknowledgements

The following materials have been reprinted by permission of their respective authors or publishers.

Robert Ashley, "And So It Goes, Depending," copyright (c) 1981; "Postscript to, 'And So It Goes, Depending'," copyright (c) 1986; and "The Backyard," (episode seven from "Perfect Lives"), copyright (c) 1983, Robert Ashley.

Michael Brewster, "Gone to Touch," copyright (c) 1987, Michael Brewster.

Herbert Brün, "On Anticommunication," copyright (c) 1988, Herbert Brün; "Snow," copyright (c) 1984, Herbert Brün.

John Cage, "C B C Interview re Bach with Ann Gibson," copyright (c) 1988, Univerity Press of America; and, excerpt from the Forward of *M*, copyright (c) 1973 by John Cage. Reprinted from *M* by permission of Wesleyan University Press.

Alvin Curran, "Maritime Rites * The Lake," copyright (c) 1988, University Press of America.

Thomas DeLio, "Untitled (Sound Installation)," copyright (c) 1988, Thomas DeLio.

David Dunn, "Madrigal: The Language of the Environment is Encoded in the Patterns of its Living Systems," copyright (c) 1988; and, "An Expository Journal of Extractions from Wilderness," copyright (c) 1988, David Dunn.

Kenneth Gaburo, "Show Tellies: Video Compositions," copyright (c) 1976; and "Rethink," copyright 1987, Lingua Press, reprinted by permission.

Ron Kuivila, "Sound Installations," copyright (c) 1988, University Press of America.

Alvin Lucier, "Seesaw," copyright (c) 1987, Alvin Lucier.

Max Neuhaus, "Max Neuhaus - Sound Installations, Techniques and Processes: The Work for the Bell Gallery at Brown University with Asides and Allusions," copyright (c) 1988, Max Neuhaus.

R. Murray Schafer, "Language, Music, Noise, Silence," copyright (c) 1988, University Press of America; excerpts from "Dicamus et Labyrinthos" (c) 1984; and "Ariadne," copyright (c) 1985, R. Murray Schafer.

Stuart Saunders Smith, "Tunnels," copyright (c) 1982 Sonic Art Editions; excerpts from "Some Household Words," copyright (c) 1983, Sonic Art Editions; and excerpts from "Poem II" and "Poems I, II, III," copyright (c) 1982, Somers Music Publications.

We want to thank the Graduate School of the University of Maryland for its financial support.

We also want to thank Jane Gethmann for all her help in preparing this manuscript.

# Table of Contents

# Introduction

At the heart of any important compositional life is the passion to transform the world. Significantly, in the present century, many composers have employed common, everyday sonic materials as the substance of their transformations. In the words of John Cage:

> Wherever we are, what we hear is mostly noise. When we listen to it, we find it fascinating. The sound of a truck at fifty miles per hour. Static between stations. Rain... There is no such thing as an empty space or an empty time. There is always something to see, something to hear... Until I die there will be sounds. And they will continue, following my death. One need not fear about the future of music.[1]

Invariably, after all upheaval and catharsis, life settles back into its previous routine. It is the routine in life that is fundamental. It is the routine that governs a culture's route and, eventually, becomes its roots. If the way one views the materials of everyday life can be altered or re-contextualized, then the most basic building blocks of a society's existence may be changed and renewed.

Toward this end, throughout the twentieth century, musicians have appropriated and explored materials drawn from environments situated outside what was previously considered the province of music; not only exploring new techniques, but also re-examining various aspects of everyday life as important compositional resources. Two of the most fundamental of such everyday sonic resources are language and space. Both are omnipresent, and both seem to be essential components in the formulation of each individual's conception of reality.

The desire to manipulate these two parameters of human existence has led to a tremendous amount of crossover among the various media. As used here, crossover, refers, not simply to the plethora of multi-media works created over the past two or three decades, in which constructions in several media are presented side-by-side, but rather, a true and profound intermingling of the fundamental elements of the various media. Thus, one finds composer's creating *sound-text* works, in which the rhythm, timbre and, often, even the content of language are used as raw materials for the creation of music. Such works are not created through any traditional processes of setting words to music, but rather, from a process of drawing music out of words. In this sense, one finds the activities and goals of the composer merging with that of the poet, and the often fine line which has separated these two media blurred, if not altogether obliterated.

Similarly, one finds another group of composers moving their work out of the concert hall in search of new environments in which to explore, experience and project sound structures. Composers of *sound-installations* tend to fix their works to the environment in much the same way that many recent sculptors have tied each of their works to the site of its presentation. Movements known as environmental-art and earth-art are a direct outgrowth of the traditional activities of sculpture. Once the pedestal was removed, sculpture naturally moved out into the environment. Following this lead, composers have also begun to root their structures in the environment. Thus, once again, the line separating different media is obliterated. As artists move out of museums and galleries into the environment, they mingle with composers who are enacting a similar process of removal from the concert hall. Sound-installations remind us that the spatial relationship between sound and auditor is of prime importance in determining the nature of the sonic experience.

There are, then, two parallel movements towards media crossover in music today: one toward domains traditionally in the province of literature; the other intermingling with, and often becoming indistinguishable from, recent examples of visual art. This anthology serves to document these two lines of development. Thus, two collections of work are actually contained herein. The first consists of a series of sound-text compositions by John Cage, Robert Ashley, Kenneth Gaburo, Herbert Brün, R. Murray Schafer, and Stuart Saunders Smith. The second consists of a series of sound-installations by Alvin Lucier, Max Neuhaus, Alvin Curran, Michael Brewster (who comes to the world of sound installations from the visual arts rather than from music), Ron Kuivila and Thomas DeLio. In addition, a hybrid work by David Dunn is included which, quite literally, draws language from the environment, thereby simultaneously blurring the boundaries which separate all three media - music, poetry and sculpture. No attempt has been made to be particularly comprehensive -a task which, under any circumstances, would be impossible. Rather, a sampling of the work of thirteen very original and important figures in these fields was compiled.

This volume is presented as a collection of primary research materials for scholars and artists. Each composer presents either a score or some form of documentation of one of his works and, in an accompanying essay, discusses his music in detail, exploring both its aesthetic and structural premises. The purpose of this book is not to present analyses or critical evaluations of this original and diverse body of works but rather, for the first time, to document the major activities of recent composers working in the important hybrid media of sound-text and sound-installation. It is hoped that this book both will mark the beginning of a general recognition of the importance of such inter-media works as well as encourage future exploration of the aesthetic and structural innovations contained therein.

In light of this, it is important to consider the relationship between the compositions included in this book and the accompanying essays, written by the composers themselves. There is much that is both logical and, at the same time, unpredictable in the creative act and a composer is really in no better position than anyone else to analyze the confluence of forces which interact to shape his own artistic endeavors. At best, he can set forth his intentions and accept - indeed, embrace - the uncertainties through which both he and his audience are led. As will be immediately apparent, the essays contained in this book are vastly different in style, structure and aesthetic import. Just as each composition is totally unique so also is each composer's essay a unique document which often complements his composition in may fascinating ways. Thus, each essay is presented more as a "mirror" of the art work than an explication of its meaning and structure. As such, the editors welcomed and, indeed, encouraged stylistic differences among the authors since such differences often provide insights into compositional differences found among the various musical works. Thus, the essays are presented as further examples of these composer's unique thought processes. As such, the essays too should be taken as primary research materials, complementing and extending the musical compositions.

The art object is a catalyst for change. In order to understand the products of any radically new approach to making art, the observer must often change his perceptual framework. Only then can he hope to make sense out of the art work. At first, the observer may experience a new work as non-sense;[2] then as he changes, he experiences a new-sense; and, eventually, it becomes a common-sense, at which point the object may cease to provide information and become, instead, mere fact. It is possible that, somewhere deeply embedded in the values of Western society lies the notion that "arriving" is not good for a culture's health and well being. Cultural health is maintained by continually travelling. By constantly enriching and transforming how we perceive the world and by continually broadening the base of possible perceptual strategies, artists provide a culture with constant sparks of renewal - a fountain of growth. The creative process begins with the artist observing himself changing in the face of newly invented sensory experience. Artistic growth (change) begins and continues with the artist changing his perception of the world as it filters through him. In gauging and evaluating this change, the artist explores new territory. He transforms and transcends his self, and like the rock thrown in the water, starts to make waves.

Perhaps the intensity of resistance to an artwork can be one measure of its success. Derek Sanders, in his book *Auditory Perception of Speech* notes:

> The more permanent the internal pattern representation is, the less dependency on the external information contained in the acoustic event. If asked to listen to a list containing familiar items (e.g. days of the week, the multiplication tables, or a well-known verse) detailed memory permits rapid identification of the pattern of the list and prediction of future items.[3]

The familiar, then permits selective attention. It is hoped that this book will provide the reader with art works which permit only full, undivided attention. It is also hoped that this collection will serve as both guide and catalyst for further inquiry into these vital areas of new music. One's daily space, one's daily words are basic to one's daily life. If composer's can transform the way relationships are perceived in space and through language, then perhaps someday, society will become radically transformed in its everyday existence.

Thomas DeLio
Stuart Saunders Smith
1987

1.       John Cage, *Silence* (Middletown, Connecticut: Wesleyan University Press, 1961), pp. 3, 8.

2.       The importance of nonsense can hardly be overstated. The more clearly we experience something as "nonsense," the more clearly we seem to be experiencing the boundaries of our own self-imposed cognitive structures. By nonsense, we mean that which does not fit into the prearranged patterns which we have superimposed upon reality. See *The Dancing Wulimasters: An Overview of the New Physics*, (New York: William Morrow and Co., Inc., 1979).

3.       Derek Sanders, *Auditory Perception of Speech*, (Englewood Cliffs, New Jersey: Prentice-Hall, 1977), pp. 152.

**Words**

Robert Ashley

ROBERT ASHLEY was born in 1930 in Ann Arbor, Michigan. He is known as a pioneer in the development of large-scale, collaborative performance works and new forms of opera. His recordings, such as *She Was A Visitor* and *In Sara, Mencken, Christ and Beethoven There Were Men and Women* and *Automatic Writing*, have pointed the way to new uses of language in a musical setting. His current trilogy of narrative works ("operas"), *Atlanta (Acts of God)*, *Perfect Lives*, and *Now Eleanor's Idea* (quartet in progress), are continuations of his long-time interest in and use of visual media in conjunction with musical ideas.

Ashley was educated at the University of Michigan and the Manhattan School of Music. Later, he worked at the Speech Research Laboratories (psychoacoustics and cultural speech patterns) at the University of Michigan. During the 1960s, he was a co-organizer of the ONCE Festival, the annual Ann Arbor festival of contemporary performing arts. He organized and toured with the ONCE Group, later the Sonic Arts Union, and directed the Center for Contemporary Music at Mills College (1969 to 1981).

During 1975 and 1976 he produced and directed his first TV opera, *Music with Roots in the Aether* (video portraits of composers and their music), which documented the work and ideas of seven major American Composers. The Kitchen in New York City commissioned *Perfect Lives*, an opera for TV, in 1978. It was purchased by The Fourth Channel (Great Britain) and completed in August, 1983.

Ashley is presently working on a 35-mm film entitled *Odalisque*, and writing a quartet of operas for stage and television. *Improvement (Don Leaves Linda)*, the first of the quartet, was part of the National Institute for Music Theater's Workshop program in 1985 and is in final development.

**As So It Goes, Depending (1980)**

about

**Perfect Lives**

An Opera-for-Television (1983)

Robert Ashley

There is always the fascination of landscape. When the piecing together of imagery becomes so intense that one is aware of its rhythms, in effect the action of the perceiving mind, "opera", or the communication of those rhythmic forms, arises naturally.

One is reluctant to orchestrate those forms without the use of words. Instrumental music is precariously "incidental" enough, even when the image it is incidental to is most commonplace or casual. One is reminded of the notion that instrumental music is incidental to speech, intrinsically and historically, most intensely, most poignantly (reminded) when the performance, or the situation of the performance (in deja-vu), gives rise to inadvertent imagery. Everyone has experienced this, composers probably more than most.

So, in the most practical and humorous sense, in the presence of an intense flow of visual rhythm, the wise composer resorts to words to slow that motion, to make intelligibility where otherwise there would be chaos. Words have a way of attaching themselves to meaning. They are the most effective pacifiers.

At certain times in life, and I suppose that this is true for some people more than for others, an irrepressible, engulfing visual imagery dominates the consciousness, almost to the point of requiring relief. This is the story one has to tell.

I tried first to attach to the image flow an inconsequential word pattern, to pretend that it didn't matter, to open a correspondence with someone ("Dear George. . ."). The imagery was so powerfully present that I fell for the illusion of its immediacy. I believed in a cure. In part, I believe, I wrote (typed) because there was no musical instrument handy to me (for maybe the first time in my life), and I was confused because my habits for using up "energy" had had to change so drastically. This was four years ago. After a while of this, it came to me gradually that I was only typing what I had rehearsed again and again in speech. In other words, I was talking to myself and typing for no reason in particular, or at least for no reason related to the talking.

I discovered that I could sort out in the piles of typed paragraphs those that had come from different rhythmic sources, and by that I mean paragraphs of repetitions of certain simple phrases in a variety of different word combinations, some of which made sense and others not so much --- even without finding anywhere the rhythmic "germ" itself (e.g. " ' there is something *y*' can always count on, *A*lice gets the bl*a*me"). I suppose poets have this down to a science, and I have just invented the wheel, but maybe it's not that simple.

There is a hard line between speaking and singing, hard to find, but hard, nevertheless, imposed from somewhere. It is an obligation. Studying it or where it is teaches us something. It keeps moving "toward" speech, at least in our time, but the quality of the line and the quality of the obligation have not changed, and, so, depending which side of the line you put your work, for whatever reason, you are required to find a form for what amounts to ranting (which violates the line and is against the law, therefore) either in the world of music, or, I can only suppose, in whatever the other world calls itself (poetry?).

In the case of *Perfect Lives* there is from the point of view of a composer a special "problem", which has its history in the movement of the "line" toward speech. The tendency enriches music, obviously, and at the same time makes old fashioned many of the given ideas about "setting" words to music, because speech is, in general, both more dense than what could be married to music in the past and more subtle. To put it in another way, as your listening changes, speech (itself) more and more seems to *be* music, and the notion of the setting as a leisurely accompaniment, detached and perhaps symbolic, is less and less useful.

The problem is not, thankfully, aesthetic. I mean, its roots are not in "the law", or social inequities, or whatever. The problem is technical, or technological, in the sense that it has to do with the machinery of making music and the machinery for listening to music, which are always two parts of the same.

My taste is to want every sound to be amplified electronically. I have lost my taste for mechanical amplification, acoustical instruments and acoustical halls. I have lost my taste for the tempo of mechanical life and its representation in, say, vocal projection. I like sounds that formerly were too soft or too short or too quick to be useful. In any tradition those sounds, to the degree that they are recognized, are called nuance. They are recognized as attachments to a main form. Now, we are all in a blizzard of nuance, so dense that a main form, supposing it's there at all, is lost.

Speaking aesthetically, now, I have imagined *Perfect Lives* as a perfect song: that is, all song; that is, not requiring a setting or an accompaniment. But at the same time I always want the densest texture of nuance I can get away with. Density is a real factor and an enjoyment for me. I am not prepared to do the perfect song with my voice (who is?), nor am I willing to slow things down so that nuance becomes a lesson. It is hard, if not impossible, for real desnity of nuance or detail to be done singularly, even allowing for multiplying oneself electronically. The presence becomes repetitious and redundant. Real density is modeled on society, where differentiation is a supreme value. (Long preamble to the invention of another wheel).

The nature of the collaboration in every aspect of the composition of *Perfect Lives* is that I could not do it alone, as I have said. It is, in my way of thinking, aesthetically impossible. It is *required* that *Perfect Lives* represent as many voices as it can sustain. Ideally, these separate voices should be as distinguishable as the technique will allow. Ideally, they should be without restriction as to their detail (amount). They are independent and simultaneous. The technique requires them to be synchronous. Otherwise, they are separate, private parts (joke).

The hierarchy of those parts, the priority of their appearance, comes from complicated, practical causes; obviously, there needn't (or shouldn't) be a hierarchy, as such. The idea is old fashioned and suggests "accompaniment". But, in fact, the possibility of planning and organizing the production of the piece so that "all things are equal" requires the assurance of a way of working (read: "money") that is not given to me. I have to work one step at a time, so there is, *a priori*, a priority (joke).

First came the text, or the perfect song. In working on *Perfect Lives* I was able, almost for the first time, to direct speech, or the sound of myself talking to myself, into specific forms. In other words, to compose (after whatever is that period of time or accumulation of unbidden materials that allows the materials to make "intentions" recognized.) Those forms, in turn, were attached to (imitations of) the categories of the imagery that caused the words in the first place. These attachments or imitations I have called, because the meaning of the word is essentially visual, "templates".

The template has two aspects. One is the metrical and rhythmic definition of the text ("repetitions of certain simple phrases in a variety of different word combination, some of which make sense of others not so much.") The other is the assembly of the short units of the text into the form of the episode. This sense of the

7

use is perhaps more trivial. It simply describes the way the episode is put together in "blocks" so that the narrative has cadences and points of synchronization among the "parts". On the other hand, it gives each of the episodes an (almost) arbitrary external "form" that certainly makes narrative, such as it is, clearer. In other words, most of the paragraphs about a certain image (and, thus, in a certain metrical and rhythmic template) are grouped together. And, further, (arbitrarily) paragraphs can be added or deleted to make the episodes have a uniform length. (Maybe not so trivial.)

But the first step in the hierarchy, the creation of the first character in the opera, was the creation of the language that imitates the imagery. At this stage in the work I am still daydreaming. The gap between the language and the actuality of sound is enormous. The job: 1) stay awake; 2) create density.

In *Perfect Lives* there are no "melodies" or "harmonies" or other traditional devices prescribed. There are only *characters* or, more specifically, individual performers telling the same story, as embodied in the templates, synchronously. In other words, there are no melodies other than the melodies invented by "Blue" Gene Tyranny (as "Buddy", the piano player) to characterize "piano playing" or the melodies invented by the singers to give nuance to the story telling. Nor are there harmonies other than the harmonic plan designed by "Blue" Gene to accommodate his improvisations in an equal-tempered keyboard style. (When new kinds of keyboards come into use, I think this element could change radically, but maybe that's stretching the point.)

In other words, the process of composing the details of the parts (characters) begins with collaboration and agreement in the recording studio and ends (never ends) only in performance. This point is essential to the piece. I haven't composed melodies or harmonies or entrances or orchestration, because I have found that approach difficult precisely in the area of story telling or "opera" in that the product of that approach is archetypically a revisionist history, rooted in memory and prejudice, and restricts the composer to speaking about the past only (or, apparently so, considering the contemporary repertoire). The idea of story telling modeled on the technology of the electronic media, a gathering of actualities, seems more relevant, bypassing the past, and interesting to me.

The techniques of the traditional role for the composer seem to me inextricably involved in maintaining the past as a field of understanding, i.e., "modernism". I find the idea of a single vision, the idea of the "auteur", incompatible with the demands of maintaining a mode of actuality. A technique of profound

8

collaboration is essential. In the blizzard (see above) the composer should rather be the instigator and the guide than the model and the definition. The idea of a profound collaboration suggests, to me, relinquishing every eminent domain in favor of actuality and relevance. So, by "collaboration" I do not mean just bringing together the various elements of 19th century music drama (text/music/costumes/decor/lighting/direction/concessions/etc.), though, God knows, you can't know everything. I mean mutual involvement in the evanescent aspects of the materials, such as they are today, and specifically in the case of opera in the music itself. (A typical case of why ranting is against the law).

Where was I? The point is that to approach the kind of density that I like I wanted to involve as many simultaneous characters in the form of actual musical personalities (i.e., performers inventing independently) as the piece could sustain. And I allow that should the personalities change, the outcome would change as drastically as when a jazz ensemble changes players, say.

So, without "Blue" Gene Tyranny, Jill Kroesen, David Van Tieghem and Peter Gordon there is no "music" to speak of. That is, the density is not what is required in my imagination of the piece. (The visual collaboration is another story, no less complicated.)

To go back to the working process, the "story" of *Perfect Lives* the source of the imagery and the musical inspiration, is recounted, not enacted. The story takes place "off stage", like the stories in the TV Evening News. The connection between the characters and the events of the story and the existential reality of the performance is in the illusion of the appearance of the characters as performers and in the use of video imagery to illustrate the locales and the moods through which the story passes. This technique, the "connection", uses various devices and degrees of illusionism based on *naming* of characters (as such) and on the tonality of nuance adopted by the singers and the pianist. In other words, the performers *change* character through the techniques of nuance and naming.

"Blue" Gene's action is the least changing. The act of keyboard playing is so complex an image that almost any illusion of character substitution is precluded. This is not to suggest that "Blue" Gene is not "telling the story" in his performance, but rather that there is hardly room in that performance for any other character than "Buddy". On the other hand, or for the same reason, "Buddy" is the most *real* character and the most complex. That is, in the amount of detail shown, this part requires the most characterization.

9

I have seen "Blue" Gene do miracles along this line, but on a schedule of six nights a week, only God . . . it is said. So, there are stored on tape other keyboard parts, composed by "Blue" Gene, which can be combined to make up a kind of grand keyboard, of which his live invention is only a part.

The live invention is designed, of course, both in the sense of "Blue" Gene's *experience* with the musical materials in each episode and, in the "operatic" sense, designed to bring the characterization of each episode to the physical gestures, apparent to the camera, that portray "Buddy" through the templates, e.g., in *The Living Room* (Episode Five), the character of which is the "two-shot" and the template of which is the division of the picture surface into equal vertical volumes, all of "Blue" Gene's invention is in parallel hand movements (seen from above.)

Also on tape, and to the same purpose, are a number of vocal parts and rhythmic parts (principally "orchestrated" rhythms derived from the accompaniment unit of the "Palace Organ" manufactured by the Gulbransen company. This extraordinary electronic instrument, generously made available to the project just as we had begun the studio recording sessions, is both the source of many of the keyboard parts on tape and the rhythmic foundation for the "measurement" of the templates.)

It is an important technical point that the materials on the prerecorded tape should seem, for the purposes of illusion (that is, for the purpose of the relationship of what is seen to what is heard), an illusionistic *amplification* of the characters on stage only. That is, in the setting of the telling of the story, *The Perfect Lives Lounge*, there is no hidden orchestra. There is just "the four of us . . ." What *is* hidden is the technique of the illusion, which is the day to day invention of the *amplification* of the characters on stage. The relationship of the parts on tape to the live invention among the performers is not fixed. Parts appear and disappear according to (and in "inspiration of") the performer's invention. In other words, the opera has a fifth character: the audience in *The Perfect Lives Lounge*, the active perceiver of the illusion. This role (job) is given to Peter Gordon, the musical producer on the opera project. He decides how the materials on the prerecorded tape are used. He is assisted in this by Marc Grafe in the live performances on tour. (Postscript: the final mixing of the television recording of *Perfect Lives* was done by Paul Shorr.)

The illusion, the active transformation of the performers' parts, serves to move the audience attention among the performers, to isolate the performers in their

10

roles. This is a large case of some number of people talking to themselves. The largeness is in the miracle of the common-ness of the topic. They are (all) more or less talking about the same story. How is this possible? That they are all talking more or less in harmony is another part of it. Will wonders never cease? And, finally, apparently, they don't know we're here, watching, listening. How embarrassing.

Above each character or pair of characters -- most of the characters in *Perfect Lives* are of a pair, and on stage there is a "couple" that is (apparently) all pairs -- there is a kind of thought balloon or television set, depending on whatever.

Clearly, they are in a dream. (How embarrassing.) They think they are on television. They think that between them and the audience (?) there is the intervention of some form of electronic translation of intent that can reduce rhetoric to an almost molecular scale. They are not moving. They have forgotten something. They have forgotten distance. They have forgotten size. They think that they can think and it will be heard. They look at the camera and it looks at them. Singly. They don't look at each other. They look at the television monitor and it looks at them.

The thought balloons materialized as video tapes show us (the audience) the templates themselves, the graphic imagery and camera dynamics upon which the songs are modeled. We all dream in camera movements, now, inevitably. What did we do before the zoom, the pan, the tilt, the telephoto? In the pre-lens eras how were the pictures framed in our imaginations? ("giordano bruno comes to mind, whoever he is").

There is always in collaboration the question of expertise, the question of the communication of shared experience. I am not a photographer. I am aggressively (with myself) not a photographer. Somewhere in the past, on account of an almost uninterrupted series of collaborations with camera experts, I decided that I couldn't work the camera. (How Kodak strives to break the spell of imaginary seeing, to make it practical.) ("giordano bruno's shot.").

So there is the problem of the authority of the templates manifested in reality; specifically, the problem of substitution, or what to look at with the eyes, if the pictures that give rise to the music language are in the mind only; the problem of the aesthetics of illustration; the problem of the retreat from theater and its representationism (into illustrations of actualities); the problem of the television

11

power of baseball or any other reality ("live from . . .") over sit-com without familiar faces: the problem of where to point the camera.

I decided that in this area (problem) it is wise not to put the problem on TV people. They are by definition on the very battle line between modernism (dreaming of the past) and what comes after, if anything. It's wise not to bother them. They have other problems.

I have, in fact, bothered artists who have no vested interest in television, but who *watch* TV. The problem of substitution, or what to look at with the eyes, is, for me, the problem of *finding* imagery (as in finding sounds in the recording studio, because they are no where else to be found) that does not mis-illustrate. In other words, at every point along the line of constructing an illustration of the source image (on tape) there have to be materials "around" that equal, in the variety of their usefulness and application, the materials one *finds* in the recording studio. Visualizers have been slow, on the whole, to allow themselves this art. One hopes that electronics for pictures will pick up the pace somewhat. In the meantime, not electronically, I am working with Mary Ashley and Jackie Humbert, who are excellent in making things to look at where there were none.

Technique is no problem. Technology can satisfy the rules faster than they can be made. A famous television engineer said to me, "There is no picture I can't bring up to TV standards". Why, just last night I saw pictures from Iran that apparently were composed of every fifth scan at best. Boy, they were beautiful.

So, it's pure aesthetics, the question of substituting illustration, which is "evanescent" (i.e., timely) for representation, which is burdened with intent. I like the feeling of first decisions, unreconsidered, un"cut". Music has evolved (or not lost) this technique, reluctantly, and in music it is a "standard", however bizarrely applied, e.g., "He made the Beethoven come alive."

In television only the awesome power of our fascination with "sports" has held back the death grip of the film mentality. Still, every year we face a new round of British Drama or some other poisonous replacement for fun by dopes who are, I guess, too tired at night to see what they have put on TV for us. The argument is that "people watch". The fact is: what else is there to do? The fact is: real-time is more difficult (read: "money"). But the evidence is that real-time is the greatness of TV. Mythical slob drinking beer on Sunday afternoon is not watching baseball, he's watching television. Each and every decision is a pure thrill. Carson is King for a reason.

12

So, the "problem" in *Perfect Lives* is to make something that is not finished, to make something that always has the form of first decision, unreconsidered, un"cut".

The "vision", which is the template, is a dynamic one. Every time I look again the picture has changed. That's why the paragraphs are so short. That's why the image upon which the episode is based doesn't tell the story, or have eventfulness. It is, the image, an illustration only of some deeper image that has meaning that is (probably) inherited, or passed on.

So, almost any picture will do, as long as it fits the template, which is dynamic: the pan (or "seeking"), the aggressive zoom (or "domination"), the tile (or "wonder" or "detachment"), the zoom out (or "rhetoric"), the two-shot (or "study"), the telephoto (or "confusion of the senses" or "illusionism" in its pure form), the truck (or "daydream"). See what I mean?

I have two collaborators in this: Carlota Schoolman, technically the producer, and actually one of the founders of video art: and John Sanborn, director, cameraman and video artist, who is very generous with his imagination.

Ideally, we will assemble seven isotapes for each episode, which for the decision maker, the Television Director, should present the same opportunities (for glory and for mistakes) as the average home game. Actually, (depending on the budget) four isotapes and three cameras would be best, but I will settle for the seven isotapes: three that are "illustrations" of the various domains of the characters in performance (e.g., The Narrator, "R"; The Piano Player, "Buddy"; and "The Couple", sung by Jill Kroesen and David Van Tieghem, that changes by episode) --- that is, "illustrations" of the locales of the story, some inhabited and some not, in a variety of detail. And a fourth tape that simply illustrates the text itself, in case things musical get too thick and the words are hard to understand. The other three inputs, whether cameras or tapes, are of the characters themselves, playing and singing, i.e., the action, live from the *Perfect Lives Lounge*.

I suppose that, eventually, the decisions in cases like this will be left to the TV audience itself. It seems to be moving in that direction. But for now a television version of *Perfect Lives (Private Parts)* will be a "performance" for the person, the TV Director, who has the ingredients of the story at his/her fingertips, so to speak.

If the audience is not at home, with its seven television sets and matching transponders or its effects-switcher and wall-size monitor, then, ideally, in "live" performance there should be a comparable distancing of the action from the observer(s). "Blue" Gene, Jill and David and the Narrator are playing to the cameras

13

and their monitors. It is purposeful to me to present an audience with the same amplification of *apparent distance* between the "image", filtered through the template, and the source of the manifestation of that image (the monitor) as I experienced in allowing the "image" to be amplified, in time, in the text; that is, in the manifestation of the text in sound.

This is my idea of opera or television, depending.

It didn't turn out that way of course. Money was the problem. Even though
the opera project was fully prepared and ready for production through (1) funding
from state and federal agencies and (2) four years of extensive touring in performance
(and in this way subsidized in large part by the participating artists themselves,
because the touring constitutes a kind of continuous rehearsal and development, not
well paid and physically agonizing), no American television system was even vaguely
responsive to the proposal. Initial contacts with PBS (The Petroleum Broadcasting
System) came to nothing and in fact got to be so embarrassing (with the specific PBS
affiliate increasingly trying to exploit the reputation of the project for its own fund-
raising purposes) that I finally stopped answering the phone. A Vice-President (in
charge of "special projects") for a major network told me (*verbatim*), "I wouldn't try
to put opera on (this network), if I had God playing the lead . . ." and then, "My job
is to make *dreck* for Middle-America." When I suggested that *I* was from "middle-
America" (whatever that is!) and that it was my impression that middle-America
might be less than happy with the "dreck" (in spite of what we are led to believe from
the "surveys," I know dozens of ordinary people who have virtually stopped watching
TV, except for sports and news, and quite a few families who *no longer own a
television set*: this is no exaggeration!), our conversation moved toward a quick
conclusion.

So, the production and postproduction funding for *Perfect Lives* came from
Channel Four in Great Britain, for which I have to be *amazed* and grateful. (Again,
parenthetically, with regard to the prospects of continuing to develop from the
example of *Perfect Lives* a relationship between the performing arts and the major
media of this century, the bounty for American artists from Europe's deep and
enduring interest in the contemporary world is beginning to "dry up". The work on
*Perfect Lives* put me in contact with most of the major European Broadcasters and
they are increasingly explicit in their resistance to (1) the avalance *dreck*, (2) the
frustration of producing programs by Americans that will never be seen in America
and (3) the one-way street colonialism of American producers toward the European
audience: "we will send you our old and worn out prints of 1970's murder series, but
we don't want any of your best work on our TV --- foreign accents, difference of
opinion, that stuff; you understand, right?"

For me, then, the irony of this postscript report on *Perfect Lives* is that, while I have produced (outside of the "industry") two opera-for-television projects (*Music With Roots in the Aether*, 1976, and *Perfect Lives*, 1983, the first of which has been played for tens of *thousands* of persons in closed-circuit and on minor, cable broadcasts, and the second of which has been broadcast in "Prime Time" twice in Great Britain and once on Austrian Television, with rather flattering reviews), the prospects of either of them being seen by American audiences are still virtually minimal; *and*, while I am still convinced that the future for American "opera" must involve the marriage of that genre to television --- and following in that conviction I have two more projects "in the works": the one is totally ready except for production, and the second is in rehearsal and should be finished within 1986 -- the possibility of any of that happening in collaboration with the "industry" is so dismal that sometimes (the "bad days") it seem like a form of insanity in me to go on. The situation is really desperate. We are all embarrassed that our children can see the most disgusting examples of mythical violence (laced with racial and sexists stereotypes) at any time of the day or night --- the only difference being that at night they are "newer" and the advertising is more expensive --- but we have no recourse. The simple truth is that the Vice-President I spoke to is *not* making dreck for middle-America; she is making it for the "industry", which apparently is so bureaucratically self-absorbed and self-serving (and so tired and drunk at night from the continuing negotiations) that it doesn't even watch what it is producing. They hire people to do that! And meanwhile, over at PBS, the British Empire continues to crumble.

I *assert*, against what almost anybody in the "industry" will contradict, that any major series of programs *about* contemporary music (on a larger scape of conception than the record promos on MTV), commissioned, produced and "promoted" with just average financing --- but not in the 1950's "documentary" style --- would be a *great success* by "industry" standards. (That it might be a "service" to our society, suggesting to us all that Americans do something besides kill each other, is beside the point.) Compare, for instance, say, *Peter the Great* or *Lord Mountbatten*. What were the budgets? $12,000,000? $14,000,000? *Peter the Great* was a turd of the first magnitude. *Nobody* I know --- young, old, in the arts or not --- would admit that they could "get through" one Episode. Do not believe what you read in TV Guide! We are into back-scratching at the point of bankruptcy. *Lord Mountbatten*? Even my wife, whose devotion to Jane Austin and the consequences has produced a proprietary curiosity about the Fall of Empire, could not get through a single Episode of that one. Unfortunately, these are not exceptional failures (as in "everybody make a mistake sometime"); they are run-of-the-mill, without-recourse, what's-on-TV: if you don't like it, watch the thirtieth-year of re-runs of *The Honeymooners*. (May the God of TV forgive me; where are the new Honeymooners, now that we need them?)

The second part of the assertion is that, if I had the chance to spend $14,000,000, a *lot of people* would watch and they wouldn't be embarrassed, either. Why must I presume to say this (?) --- that as a white person I'm embarrassed by the return of "Amos 'n Andy" in all of its manifestations. I know many black musicians. I watch, on TV, the great heroes of sports. Nobody behaves (or talks!) like what the *dreck* has given us. Walter Payton doesn't talk like that. Reggie Jackson doesn't talk like that. Kareem Abdul-Jabar doesn't talk like that. Miles Davis doesn't talk like that. Nobody talks like that, except in street-jive in outright satire of our blatant racism. So, for the moment, more important even than the prospects for *Perfect Lives* is the question of who is responsible for those programs and how can we get them imprisoned for their crimes against our society?

I want $14,000,000 (or more) to produce my own work and to commission and produce a major "music drama" by, say, Miles Davis --- where to stop? I can name one-hundred composers of *genius*, who get by on a hand-to-mouth basis and who watch only sports on TV --- but my chances of this happening are, obviously, almost zero. End of sermon.

*Perfect Lives*? Four isotapes, three cameras, selective story telling, passing inspiration at the switcher? It just couldn't be. I didn't give up anything of the *idea* of *Perfect Lives*, but we did it in the garage, as it were. John Sanborn (Director) *internalized* every "image" of the text (the necessity clearly made him *sick*, probably damaged his mind semi-permanently and didn't pay well at all, but you know how those artists are) and then made *one* choice from whatever huge number there may have been --- just for him! --- and made *live-TV* from materials that were only barely still "alive". It was like that scene from *Gone With the Wind* where they are trying to keep about four hundred extras alive until the lunch break. Except that for us (John Sanborn, Dean Winkler, Paul Shorr and me) the "scene" lasted for about ten months and was enacted almost always at night, which is when human beings should be sleeping or having a party. We went to the studio at about 6 (PM) and came home, on lucky days at about 6 (AM). At my age I might have died. (How charming!) When we finished, I was so tired in all of myself that my coordination was impaired. In Boston they would have accused me of being drunk. In Oakland the guys in the

17

squad car, having seen me, would have circled the block, just to check. Fortunately, we were working in New York, where there is enough diversity that most people get the idea. It took me about six months to learn to sleep again. (Never mind "dreaming" --- I learned to do that standing up.) But *Perfect Lives* was actually *finished*. An opera-for-television in seven, half-hour episodes. I think it is wonderful. It is an example of --- it would be deceitfully greedy of me to be modest about this point -- at least "genius" and maybe even almost perfect execution on the part of everybody involved (possibly me excluded, on account of the accumulated fatigue), as in a non-hit game.

Thanks to the unflagging trust in the project on the part of Carlota Schoolman and Mary MacArthur, representing the Kitchen Center for Video Music and Dance (NYC), Mimi Johnson, Jane Yockle, and Barbara Mayfield, representing Performing Artservices, Inc. (NYC) and, finally, Andy Park and Michael Kustow, representing Channel Four (Great Britain), we got an opera-for television on TV (somewhere). I think a lot of people liked it.

As for U.S.A. -- well, we might have to wait until the actors in the prime-time programs have to start using real bullets (ratings, you known). In the meantime, in the spirit of *Perfect Lives*, keep watching baseball, golf, late night sex and all of those programs about animals where nothing of any particular "importance" seems to be about to happen. As soon as you feel that first tingle of *threat* in any other kind of program (the threat, which is the sugar of our junk culture and which, I think, is the same as the "instinct" to cross the street, when you see another human approaching on your side,) change channels immediately. Tell everybody you know. Good luck.

*The Backyard*
**Episode Seven**
**from**
*Perfect Lives, an opera for television*


| *Intro* | *two* | *three* | *four* | *five* | *six*

| *seven* | *eight* | *nine* | *ten* | *eleven* | *twelve*

| *thirteen* | *fourteen* | *fifteen* | *sixteen* | *seventeen* | *eighteen*

| *nineteen* | *twenty* | *twenty-one* | *twenty-two* | *twenty-three* | *twenty-four*

| *twenty-five* | *twenty-six* | *twenty-seven* | *twenty-eight* | *twenty-nine* | *thirty*

| *thirty-one* | *thirty-two* | *thirty-three* | *thirty-four* | *thirty-five* | *thirty-six*

| *thirty-seven* | *thirty-eight* | *thirty-nine* | *forty* | *forty-one* | *forty-two*

| *forty-three* | *forty-four* | *forty-five* | *forty-six* | *forty-seven* | *forty-eight Section*

| *A five count* | *two* | *three* | *four* | *five*
| *           She makes a double life.

| *two*           She makes two from one and one.

| *three*           She makes a perfect system every day.

| *four*           She makes it work.

| *five*           She stands there in the doorway of her mother's house

| *six*           looking at the grass and sky and at where they meet,

| *seven*           never once thinking thoughts like

| *eight*           it's so like a line,

| *nine*           or, the difference is so powerful,

| *ten* | *two* | *three* | *four* | *five My*
| *           or, which way shall I take to leave.

| *mind five count* | *two* | *three* | *four* | *five*
| *                         My mind turns to my breath, one.

| *two*                     My mind watches my breath, two.

| *three*                   My mind turns and watches my breath, three.

| *four*                    My mind turns and faces my breath, four.

| *five*                    My mind faces my breath, five.

| *six*                     My mind studies my breath, six

| *seven*                   My mind sees every aspect of the beauty of my breath, seven.

| *eight*                   My mind watches my breath soothing itself, eight.

| *nine*                    My mind sees every part of my breath, nine.

| *ten* | *two* | *three* | *four* | *five Section*
| *                         My breath is not indifferent to itself, ten.

| *B five count* | *two* | *three* | *four* | *five*
| *                         She never thinks of possibility

| *two*                     or of how probable it is that they have come together.

| *three*                   Those thoughts never enter her mind.

| *four*                    Nor do thoughts of sports.

| *five*                    She has no desire to improve her muscles.

| *six*                     For her, piano playing is the only mystery.

| *seven*                   It's so beautiful, and how they do it no one knows.

| *eight*      She gets catalogues of every sort in the mail.

| *nine*      Everything imaginable is pictured.

| *ten*      She finds her way among the pictures without hesitation.

| *eleven*      Happiness is just around the corner.

| *twelve*      She is entirely without shame.

| *thirteen*      The numbers are made of rubber or something like that.

| *fourteen*      They stretch.

| *fifteen*      They never lose their shape.

| *sixteen*      They are ageless.

| *seventeen*      They don't need repair.

| *eighteen* | *two* | *three* | *four* | *five Section*
| *      They need attention and respect.

| *C six count* | *two* | *three* | *four* | *five* | *six*
| *      She thinks about two things that I know of.

| *two*      One is elevation,

| *three*      and that comes clothed in light, so to speak.

| *four*      She loathes the dark.

| *five*      She sleeps in light.

| *six*      She likes highness.

| *seven*      Four thousand one hundred twenty-eight feet here.

| *eight*          Four thousand two hundred eighteen feet there.

| *nine*           And the body of the house itself.

| *ten*            Fourteen dollars and twenty-eight cents here.

| *eleven*         Forty-eight dollars and twelve cents there.

| *twelve*         The other is proportions.

| *thirteen*       Coincidence isn't a mystery to her.

| *fourteen*       The margin is always wide enough.

| *fifteen*        Forty-two or forty with twenty is always sixty-two or sixty.

| *sixteen*        And I mean forty-two with twenty can be sixty as well as sixty-two.

| *seventeen*      And the other way around.

| *eighteen*       Just as ten and twenty can be thirty-two or thirty.

| *nineteen*       Or twelve and twenty can be thirty.

| *twenty*         She stands there in the doorway of her mother's house and thinks
                   these thoughts.

| *twenty-one*     That fourteen dollars and twenty-eight cents is more attractive than
                   fourteen dollars,

| *twenty-two*     because of the twenty-eight.

| *twenty-three*   No one likes or dislikes zeros.

| *twenty-four* | *two* | *three* | *four* | *five* | *six* Section
| *               And that forty-two or forty is fixed, in some way.

| *D five count* | *two* | *three* | *four* | *five*
| *                She thinks about her father's age.

| *two*            She does the calculations one more time.

| *three*          She remembers sixty-two.

| *four*           Thirty and some number is sixty-two.

| *five*           And that number with ten is forty-two.

| *six*            She remembers forty-two.

| *seven*          Remembers is the wrong word.

| *eight*          She dwells on forty-two.

| *nine*           She turns and faces it.

| *ten*            She watches.

| *eleven two* | *three* | *four* | *five Section*
| *                She studies it.

| *E five count* | *two* | *three* | *four* | *five*
| *                It is the key.

| *two*            The mystery of the balances is there.

| *three*          The masonic secret lies there.

| *four*           The church forbids its angels entry there.

| *five*           The gypsies camp there.

| *six*            Blood is exchanged there.

| *seven*          Mothers weep there.

23

| *eight*      It is night there.

| *nine*       Thirty and some number is sixty-two.

| *ten*        And that number with ten is forty-two.

| *eleven*     That number translates now to then.

| *twelve*     That number is the answer, in the way that numbers answer.

| *thirteen* | *two* | *three* | *four* | *five*
| *           That simple notion, a coincidence among coincidences is all one

              needs to know.

| *Mind five count* | *two* | *three* | *four* | *five*
| *           My mind turns to my breath.

| *two*        My mind watches my breath.

| *three*      My mind turns and watches my breath.

| *four*       My mind turns and faces my breath.

| *five*       My mind faces my breath.

| *six*        My mind studies my breath.

| *seven*      My mind sees every aspect of the beauty of my breath.

| *eight*      My mind watches my breath soothing itself.

| *nine*       My mind sees every part of my breath.

| *ten* | *two* | *three* | *four* | *five* Section
| *           My breath is not indifferent to itself.

| *F five count* | *two* | *three* | *four* | *five*
| *            She waked at ten.

| *two*            She remembers ten.

| *three*            She left the dark at ten.

| *four*            She waked in light.

| *five*            So forty-two or forty or forty-four is fixed.

| *six*            Fourteen dollars and twenty-eight cents is more attractive than

fourteen dollars.

| *seven*            It's just that way.

| *eight* | *two* | *three* | *four* | *five In-*
| *            The firmness of it is a consolation.

|*sert six count* | *two* | *three* | *four* | *five* | *six*

| *two* | *two* | *three* | *four* | *five* | *six*

| *three* | *two* | *three* | *four* | *five* | *six Section*

| *G six count* | *two* | *three* | *four* | *five* | *six*
| *            Three men have loved her.

| *two*            One a decade on the average.

| *three*            Uncertainties are wrong.

| *four*            In this scene there is one shot.

| *five* | *two* | *three* | *four* | *five* | *six Section*
| *            Giordano Bruno comes to mind, whoever he is.

| *H six count* | *two* | *three* | *four* | *five* | *six*
| *                     She is in the doorway of her mother's house.

| *two*                 She faces south.

| *three*               We see it two ways.

| *four*                First is the house behind her and the great northern constellations.

| *five*                She looks away from difference and discrepancy.

| *six*                 Magnetic north, true north, the north star path . . .

| *seven*               It's too like the calculations.

| *eight*               Except that ten and forty-two are fixed together.

| *nine*                We are looking west.

| *ten*                 She is on the right edge of the shot.

| *eleven*              She is earth.

| *twelve*              We are the sun.

| *thirteen*            People are gathered in the backyard.

| *fourteen*            This is the celebration of the changing of the light.

| *fifteen*             They do it as often as they can in summer.

| *sixteen*             They come to talk.

| *seventeen*           They pass the time.

| *eighteen*            They soothe their thoughts with lemonade.

| *nineteen*            They say things like:

| *twenty*       She never had a stitch that she could call her own, poor thing.

| *twenty-one*   And, Carl's still president over at the bank, ain't he?

| *twenty-two*   And, now, if I was doing it . . .

| *twenty-three* And, she didn't cook much, never really had the time, you know.

| *twenty-four*  And, I wouldn't say that, not at all.

| *twenty-five*  They are the planets in this scheme of things.

| *twenty-six*   Giordano Bruno's shot.

| *twenty-seven* The problem is the arc.

| *twenty-eight* The changing angle of the shot.

| *twenty-nine*  It defies geometry.

| *thirty*       The drawings of a many-centered solar system, when we meet them in

         the books,

| *thirty-one*   make us avert our eyes.

| *thirty-two* | *two* | *three* | *four* | *five* | *six* Section
| *
         Heresy is heresy.

| *I six count* | *two* | *three* | *four* | *five* | *six*
| *
         We make one great weird curve from the east edge of the backyard

         looking west—

| *two*          she is on the right edge of the shot—

| *three*        across, following the equator of the backyard, to the west edge,

         looking east.

| *four*      Now she is on the left edge.

| *five*      At some point midway, we face,

| *six*       both looking at the center.

| *seven*     The center is between us.

| *eight* | *two* | *three* | *four* | *five* | *six* Section
| *          Except that for the purpose of the shot, or in the interests of

             economy, she doesn't move.

| *J five count* | *two* | *three* | *four* | *five*
| *          She's standing in the doorway of her mother's house.

| *two*       The doorway to the back porch.

| *three*     The backyard is the south.

| *four*      Behind her the great northern constellation rises in the majesty of its

             architecture.

| *five*      Well, maybe that's a little too much.

| *six*       Let's just say that contradictions are behind her.

| *seven*     And in the backyard, god, this set of circumstances

| *eight*     that is indescribable with our geometry.

| *nine*      A picnic of sorts.

| *ten*       A celebration of the changing of the light.

| *eleven*    And we glide through that chaos

| *twelve*          facing her,

| *thirteen*        watching her,

| *fourteen*        studying her.

| *fifteen*         Not circling her, remember.

| *sixteen*         Circling, but not circling her.

| *seventeen*       She is circling.

| *eighteen*        We are circling.

| *nineteen*        Now she is on the left edge.

| *twenty*          Caught, still, in her accounting of those three decades silently.

| *twenty-one*      She is so beautiful.

| *twenty-two*      A (quote) pre-industrial (unquote) equation.

| *twenty-three*    God, this is sentimental.

| *twenty-four* | *two* | *three* | *four* | *five Section*

| *K* five count | *two* | *three* | *four* | *five*
| *                 This is the hour of the mystery of the barnswallows.

| *two*             One, where do they go in daytime?

| *three*           Two, do they never rest?

| *four*            Three, when you buy them in the store, made in China, on the end of
                    strings,

| *five*            they do exactly what they do alive.

| *six*       Four, how is that possible?

| *seven*     The idea of the changing center is not in anything we make.

| *eight*     Our toys run down.

| *nine*      On the other hand, of course, the Chinese are said to not take

             pictures.

| *ten*       At least, not of the outside.

| *eleven*    Six of one, two times three of one, five plus one of one,

| *twelve* | *two* | *three* | *four* | *five* Section
| *          nine minus three of one, half a dozen of another.

| *L* five count | *two* | *three* | *four* | *five*
| *          It would be perfect if, as we made the great curve

| *two*       through the heavens of the backyard,

| *three*     providentially or accidentally, depending on

| *four*      your point of view, each of the planets would move exactly

| *five*      in the path and at the speed and with the purpose

| *six* | *two* | *three* | *four* | *five Section*
| *          of the expression of the other idea.

| *M six count* | *two* | *three* | *four* | *five*| *six*
| *          Maybe that's too much to wish.

| *two*       Giordano Bruno.

| *three*     I think they burned him.

| *four*        He was too positive.

| *five*  | *two* | *three* | *four* | *five* | *six Section*
| *                Fight fire with fire.

| *N six count* | *two* | *three* | *four* | *five* | *six*
| *                In this shot he is right about the larger order, whatever that means.

| *two*          There is the sun and earth and some center that they share.

| *three*        All other facts in this heaven,

| *four*         One has climbed a tree,

| *five*         Two are eating watermelon,

| *six*          One always says it's getting late,

| *seven*        One succeeded at the plant,

| *eight*        One works at the bank,

| *nine*         The specialists.

| *ten*          | *two* | *three* | *four* | *five* | *six Section*
| *                They are places hard to fix upon the memory.

| *O six count* | *two* | *three* | *four* | *five* *six*
| *                Sundown, one, the time it disappears.

| *two*          Gloaming, two, the twilight, dusk.

| *three*        Crepuscle, the twilight, three, the half-light.

| *four*         Twilight, four, pale purplish blue to pale violet, lighter than dusk blue.

| *five*         Civil twilight, until the sun is up to six degrees

| *six*    below horizon, enough light on clear days for ordinary occupations.

| *seven*    Nautical twilight, until the sun is up to twelve degrees below horizon.

| *eight*    Astronomical twilight, until the sun is eighteen degrees down, more or

less.

| *nine*    Clair de lune, five, greener and paler than dusk.

| *ten* | *two* | *three* | *four* | *five* | *six Section*
| *    Dusk, six, redder and darker than clair de lune.

| *P five count* | *two* | *three* | *four* | *five*
| *    Dear George, what's going on?

| *two* | *two* | *three* | *four* | *five*
| *    I'm not the same person that I used to be.

| *End* | *two* | *three* | *four* | *five*

| *six* | *seven* | *eight* | *nine* | *ten*

| *eleven* | *twelve* | *thirteen* | *fourteen* | *fifteen*

| *sixteen*

Herbert Brün

HERBERT BRÜN, born in 1918 in Berlin, Germany, studied at the Jerusalem Conservatory of Music and with Stefan Wolpe, Eli Friedmann, and Frank Pelleg. Further studies included work at Columbia University, New York. From 1955-61, in addition to his activities as a composer, he conducted research concerning electro-acoustics and electronic sound production in regard to their possibilities in the field of musical composition, in Paris, Cologne, and Munich. During this period he also worked as composer and conductor of music for the theater, gave lectures and seminars particularly emphasizing the function of music in society, and did a series of broadcasts on contemporary music. After completing a lecture tour through the United States in 1962, he came to the University of Illinois one year later, primarily to do research on the significance of computer systems for composition; he is presently Professor of Music there.

Herbert Brün is a member of the Computer Arts Society; is on the editorial board of the Computer Music Journal (MIT); is a member of the American Society for Cybernetics, and was editor of their Newsletter 1983-1984; and has been on the panel of judges for the NEWCOMP competition.

A record album of twelve of his compositions was released on Non Sequitur label in September 1983. Other compositions of his are available on the Opus One, CRI, and University of Illinois Experimental Music Studios labels. A book of his writings, *"my words and where I want them,"* was published by Princelet Editions in July 1986, and a book of reflections on music and use of the computer, *Uber Musik und zum Computer,* was published by G. Braun Verlag in May 1971. Herbert Brün's compositions are available from Smith Publications.

# On Anticommunication

*Cincinnati 1962*
*Urbana 1964*
*Cincinnati 1967*

Ladies and Gentlemen,

Seven years ago I saw Cincinnati for the first time. I had come here to listen to the first public performance of my third string-quartet by the LaSalle Quartet, an ensemble justly considered to be the best of its kind in the world today by most composers alive. For me this was a festival and it is understandable that I was in high spirits.

Two days before the concert, the members of the Quartet invited a number of friends to a private home where my piece was played and I was asked to answer questions about the music I had written, the compositional techniques I had used, and the message I intended to communicate through this composition. At this occasion I heard my quartet for the first time. Excited and immoderately pleased, I found all questions to be of the greatest relevance, answered them as best I could, remained in a splendid mood and all in all enjoyed everything, including myself.

A few days later the Museum invited me to contribute a 10 minute talk on the musical aspects of the general subject: *Existentialism and the Arts*. This I did not have ready in my drawer. It had to be produced overnight. This overnight production, a piece of condensed and spasmodically jumping prose, contains a passage which rises to the sentence: "A language gained is a language lost!" - A discouraging sentence, and, as a blunt statement, rather controversial. In the context, I knew what I meant by it. At the same time, however, I began wondering what it might mean outside such a context, and whether this question would be worth my while investigating. It turned out that it was, and all I shall tell you today is related to that first time in Cincinnati.

It did not take long for the sentence to grow old. Its informative impact, when it had raised questions, controversy and curiosity in my mind, was drowned by repetition as I went on thinking about it. It became a kind of slogan, and began to take on the features of a thing one can say. A thing one thinks one understands because one has *heard* it before and not because one has *thought* it before. The sentence fell under its own sentence and thus a language gained in Cincinnati, Ohio became a language lost in Urbana, Illinois. I decided to do something about it and

35

attempted what thousands of artists had attempted: namely to construct a context in which the decay of the sentence, of its words, of all the potential meanings implied by it, would be retarded.

This context, in which it was to live a little longer, could not be again the original Cincinnati piece of prose, nor could it be just a new audience elsewhere where it hadn't been heard yet. The context was to be of a more general appropriateness, if possible to be adequate for any place I can imagine, for any time I can think of. To make such an attempt is equivalent to intending to compose a piece: a piece of poetry to preserve any gained language of words, a piece of music to preserve any gained language of sound.

Briefly: I composed a context of words and sounds in which the sentence "a language gained is a language lost" would have a function that should prevent it from becoming unambiguous, communicative, from becoming just words, from getting lost too soon. The finished composition I triumphantly called *Futility 1964* and here it is.

*Futility 1964*

If you were
   not yet to understand
      the meaning that was conveyed
         to these events of sound
            it would be understandable

               For it is believable
                  that you do not yet believe
                     in hearing the sound of events
                        as they call on you
                           to create the suitable language
                             that will let you say to yourself
                           that which is said to you
                               just once and never again
                                  for the first and the last time

                                There is no second time
                                   since a language gained
                                 is a language lost

                                 And to even try
                                 to tell you this
                                     seems a sheer waste of time
                                   for it is language
                                 and thus lost

What if the saying, according to which words mean what people take them to mean, were true? And let me suggest only the first few consequences, namely those which concern all of us right here and now:

If you, for instance, were an audience which by consensus has agreed on the meaning of words, then I should have studied and learned your conventions before coming here. I ought to have scanned my notes and notions and only selected those for presentation that could be expressed with your words and your meanings. All others I should have rejected as incomprehensible for you. The result would have been that everything I say would seem to make sense to you, would sound familiar to you, would let you feel confirmed and reinforced in your feelings and probably thus really bore you to death; no matter whether all of you actually perceive the identity of deadly boredom and heroic complacency.

If, on the other hand, you were an audience, where everyone reserves the right of taking words to mean whatever anyone pleases, then my task would have consisted in doing research on this audience's structure, until I discovered the average meaning associated here with the average word: I would learn how to direct my language at a majority of individuals, who, while exercising their individual rights, are more or less unaware of their conforming in reality to a consensus which *rules* this audience instead of *having been chosen* and decided by this audience. I would turn diplomat and salesman and my talk would be a viciously apologetic melody singing of the freedom of meaning, the freedom of words for us all, and of the cozy noncommittal generosity with which I present my thoughts, not for your perusal, but for your mood and fancy, to take it or to leave it. This insidious sing-song-melody has fatally distorted the dignity and the good faith of many a speaker, an artist, a composer and many an audience.

Let me mention one more consequences, and remind you that the speaker is only one person, while the audience is a multitude. Thus it is a rare case in which an audience would say: We, either all of us by consensus, or each of us by individual choice, we take words to mean thus and thus. But we have invited this individual to speak to us, and our desire is to hear what *this* person takes words to mean. It is, you will admit, a rare case, but if the audience truly has that desire, and if the invited individual trustingly attempts to fulfill it, then a certain harmony of purpose may be expected. *The speaker* shows what *the speaker* takes words to mean; *the listeners* compare this with what *the listeners* take words to mean.

But just because of the expected harmony, and just because the readiness for liberal comparison is by no means a readiness for change, for learning, for self-reflection, such a situation usually passes without any achievement.  The audience *approves* of the meanings the speaker associates with the speaker's words, only as long as the audience approves of the thought which result from these associations.  Otherwise, the audience will call the speaker's use of language false, faulty, artificial, tendentious, distorting, unacceptable.  Here the mutual agreement and harmony of purpose *prevent* a process by which language might be *taught* to acceptably utter thoughts which seem unacceptable only because of the meanings that words are *taken* to mean.

I concede that in order to relate *established* thoughts it may be sufficient to know what the listener takes words to mean, and to form one's language accordingly.  The success of this language is then measured by the degree of its comprehensibility.  The problem of the speaker here is a problem *in* communication.  The speaker's aim consists in having a new constellation of old thoughts understood by the currently valid rules and usages.

For the presentation of *new* thoughts, however, the speaker has to *make* the words mean what they here-to-fore had not meant, thus adding to the available repertory of meanings that new meaning which is necessary for the presentation of the new thought.  The success of this language can only be measured by the degree to which it *questions the sufficiency* of meanings already associated with words, and by *the quality of the thoughts* that so become audible for the first time; at which time there is, obviously, never enough evidence available that would allow for completely correct evaluations.

Where a new thought is presented, the speaker's problem is not any longer only a problem *in* communication, but one *of* communication.  A speaker with a new thought has to solve a problem of *anticommunication*.  The syllables "anti" are used here as in antipodes, antiphony, antithesis; not meaning "hostile" or "against" but rather "juxtaposed" or "from the other side".  Anticommunication faces communication somewhat as an offspring faces its progenitor.  And just as the offspring eventually will in turn become a progenitor so will anticommunication, in time, become communication.

As this is the point where the arts, including music, come in, let me comment some more on my new useful term "anticommunication".

Anticommunication is an attempt at saying something, not a refusal of saying it. Communication is achievable by *learning from* language how to say something. Anticommunication is an attempt at respectfully *teaching* language to say it. It is not to be confused with either non-communication, where no communication is intended, or with lack of communication, where a message is ignored, has gone astray or simply is not understood. Anticommunication is most easily observed, and often can have an almost entertaining quality, if well known fragments of a linguistic system are composed into a contextual environment in which they try but fail to mean what they always had meant, and, instead, begin showing traces of integration into another linguistic system, in which, who knows, they might one day mean what they never meant before, and be communicative again.

This understanding ought to make it possible for a community of people to have a good time with either communication or anticommunication. Indeed it should be noted that the good time lasts longer with anticommunication, which leaves a lot open for the next occasion, than with communication, which puts everything neatly away on the spot.

All this I contend to be analogously the case in all systems in which the elements enter into temporarily significant coalitions, and where some communicable meaning becomes associated with either their moments of appearing or with the particular structure of their appearance. Words in language, gestures of sound in music, definitions of visual units and colors in painting are just a few of the many terms denoting such coalitions.

Every thought, idea, or concept, as it emerges for the first time in a given society, needs words so that it be expressed, be presented, be heard, understood and finally communicated. In search of such language one has to either create *new* words, or add and attach new *meanings* to old words. If a word, in the course of time and usage, has accumulated many kinds, shades, and nuances of meaning, then we have to consider the context in which the word appears in order to know which particular meaning it is to carry. From this it follows that a *new* meaning of a word may be suspected, or assumed, if the context is such that none of the *conventional* meanings would fit.

It is easier to coin and integrate a new word, a new sound, a new visual unit, than to make an old one mean something new. This is because the newly coined word announces its newness in every context. Its function is unambiguous and thus not context-bound. A new meaning on the other hand cannot be announced by an old word alone, but only by a context to which the old word is a newcomer, in which it had never functioned before. The older a word is, the more meanings it has accumulated; the more ambiguous it becomes, the more context-bound it is. Whereas a *new word* adds to the language by enlarging the vocabulary, a new *meaning* adds to the language by increasing the significance of context.

At the moment in which something new is conceived, introduced, and noticed, a temporary gap opens, an *interregnum*, which disappears only when that new something becomes accepted, understood, used, when it begins to grow old. This time of transition is a time in which messages are sent that no one receives, and in which messages are received that no one sent. This is the time in which a language gained is a language lost.

By most people this time is experienced only occasionally, in passing, in some concert, some exhibition, some reading, and then usually not too happily; for it gives them a hard time or no time or too much time, but no answer to their questions: "What does it all mean?" It is this time, however, that is the almost continuous time present for those poets, painters, and composers who move with it, who think of themselves as living and working just in that mute and dumb moment where the language they gained got lost, where it won't do and say what they would have it do and say.

It is therefore a sign of understanding and perceptivity if one expects their productions, their works and words to escape the prevalent level of communicativity; under the condition that all of their activities and objects be at least propositions and at best provisions for the next, now the future, level of communicativity. Creative Art resides in poetry, music, dance, painting, architecture, theater, film, television, writing, and even in "happenings", only if each of these sub-disciplines function by anticommunication, which is my term for potential and virtual expression in a field devoid of communicative guarantee. One ought to expect, yes, as an ambitious audience, even demand, that this field be cultivated at a time later than the last harvest and earlier than the next.

But, what if it is not only the much maligned audience, the people who come to listen and to see, who have the wrong expectations? What if it is a society itself, and therewith also the performers, the dancers, the actors, the musicians, who do not know that their profession consists in handling competently the temporary incompetence of their languages? What if they have not matured enough in order to liberate and promote language from its fictitious status of a slave who will do the best it can, to the status-independent existence of students, who will try to do better than the best anyone can?

In two different ways I have attempted to get at this problem. In your eyes, performers and musicians are somewhat nearer to composers than is society in general. I should tell you that this may be a mistake. Musicians are nearer to the composer only when they intend to introduce the composer's language as theirs, whereas they drop back into the general pool of incompetent society as soon as they merely use it as the composer's. That means that the composer must pay attention to musicians, because the composition (the work of the composer), at least in performance, depends on their paying attention to the implications of the score.

A score is a document in which a composer has specified as precisely as deemed necessary, the kind and production of acoustical events the composer wanted heard and the context in which these events would carry the musical meaning the composer wanted perceived. Just as in language, there may be new sounds that still have to gain some musical meaning for the first time; and there surely will be many old sounds, which will, in the context, begin to adopt a fresh meaning, to be substituted for, or added to the meanings that had rendered the sound a musical sound before. In studying a score one can see which degree of precision the composer has deemed necessary for the composed specifications. And from that one may conjecture and speculate extensively as to the intentions the composer probably had, in particular as to the kind of attention the composer meant to pay to the performers and the kind of attention the composer desires from them.

The upshot of all this is a proposition; or rather a chain of analogous propositions: To the question whether a statement is true there be added the question: what if it were true? - To the question whether a composition is music there be added the question: what if this were music? So that language may not become a fossilized fetish, let it be praised for the thoughts it expresses, but ruthlessly criticized for the ideas it fails to articulate. Language is not the standard against which thinking is to be measured; on the contrary: Language is to be measured by a standard it barely reaches, if ever, namely the imagery of human doubt and human desire.

To measure language, with imagery as a standard, is the function of art in society. The arts are a measuring meta-language about the language that is found wanting. If the imagery succeeds in containing, anticommunicatively, for later, the simulation, the structural analogy to that, which was found wanting, then, who knows, it may tell us, or *some*one, *some*day, with breathtaking eloquence and in then simple terms what we, today, almost speechlessly have wanted so much.

*sentences now open wide*

SNOW 1984

Herbert Brün

I

If you were
to think
that you have something
to say
to someone
who does
not know
the words
which populate the language
and poison the speech
and spread the word, the epidemic, the plague . . . . . ,

If you still were
to think
that you have something
to say
in words
to someone

## II

If only you had
    said what you had meant to say
        I might have noticed through understanding nothing
           that had I understood
               I should have misunderstood you.

               But so I understood that which you had not meant to say
               And so indeed I misunderstood you.

Consider and please reflect upon it:

    Isn't it more urgent for me to understand what you mean to say
    than merely to understand the language
      which uses you while you think you use it?

      And don't you see how the usage of language
      would condemn me to your misunderstanding
      were I not to teach each sentence
        how to instruct its words to mean that
        which I wish to say to you?

        To merely agree on language is equivalent
      with coming to a misunderstanding
    where silence curses itself
and where the end greedily swallows its causes.

III


A word
looks no way
or both ways
or even more ways than a word can say.

Certainly you are not just words
but your words are just you
more you than you see
unless you look
at least both ways.


                              Here are you.
                              Here is a word.
                                    Look!


Both of you, look at each other!
learn how to see what you say
and learn how to say the unspeakable –
        – to say     at last
                          what you see.

IV

Do not try to tell us
　　Whoever we are
　　Whoever you may be
Do not try to tell us our needs

Ask us to tell you
　　To tell you as well as we can tell
　　what we think we need
Make us tell you

Create the context wherein we would be articulate
Create the necessary context wherein
　　Whatever we happen to say
　　Will tell you what our needs are
　　　　by words
　　　　and if we find no words
　　　　by screams
　　　　and if we can not scream
　　　　by gesture
　　　　and if even gestures are out of our reach
　　　　by the manifestation of our mere existence
　　Where the fact that we are objects
　　Though we need to be subjects
　　Tells you the need which we need to know
Even if you now know it before we do.

V

Nothing was true
And so is nothing

What has been true
Is not now
And thus nothing.

The story, the sentence, the statement
can never do more than either:

describe and propose and demand
what had better be true
just because it is not,
right now not yet true;

or:

describe and propose and demand
What had better be taken for true
because it just *was* not and *is* not
and never will *be* true except in

The story, the sentence, the statement.

John Cage

JOHN CAGE was born in Los Angeles in 1912. He studied with Richard Buhlig, Henry Cowell, Adolph Weiss, and Arnold Schoenberg. In 1949 he received a Guggenheim Fellowship and an award from the National Academy of Arts and Letters for having extended the boundaries of music through his work with percussion orchestra and his invention of the prepared piano (1940). In 1951 he organized a group of musicians and engineers to make music on magnetic tape. In 1952, at Black Mountain College, he presented a theatrical event considered by many to have been the first "happening." A twenty-five year retrospective concert of his compositions was presented at Town Hall in 1958.

He is musical advisor for the Merce Cunningham Dance Company, having been associated with Merce Cunningham since 1943. Cage was elected to the Institute of the American Academy and Institute of Arts and Letters in 1968, and to the American Academy of Arts and Sciences in 1978. He has been a fellow of the Centers for Advanced Studies at Wesleyan University, the University of Cincinnati and the University of California at Davis, and was a Regent's Lecturer at the University of California at San Diego in 1980. He received an honorary degree from the California Institute of the Arts at Commencement exercises in 1986.

Recent commissions include *Thirty Pieces for Five Orchestras* (1981) for the Orchestra de Lorraine and the Centre European pour la Recherche Musicale , and *Dance/4 Occhestras* for the 1982 Cabrillo Festival, Aptos, California. *A House Full of Music* was commissioned by Radio Bremen in May, 1982. *Roaratorio, an Irish Circus on Finnegans Wake* (1979), commissioned and co-produced by the West German Radio, and the Dutch Catholic Radio, and realized in collaboration with John Fullemann in the IRCAM studios in Paris, was awarded the Karl Sczuka Prize in 1979.

Cage is the author of *Silence* (1961), *A Year From Monday* (1968), *M* (1973), *Empty Words* (1979), and *X* (1983), all published by the Wesleyan University Press; *Notations* (with Alison Knowles, 1969) published by Something Else Press; *Writing Through Finnegans Wake*, published by Printed Editions (1979); *For the Birds* (conversations with Daniel Charles, 1981) published by Marian Boyars; *Another Song* (accompanying photographs by Susan Barron) and *Mud Book Themes and Variations* published by the Station Hill Press, 1982.

# Some Words From M

## John Cage

Reading the *Journal*, I have been struck by the twentieth-century way Thoreau listened. He listened, it seemed to me, just as composers using technology nowadays listen. He paid attention to each sound, whether it was "musical" or not, just as they do; and he explored the neighborhood of Concord with the same appetite with which they explore the possibilities provided by electronics. Many of my performances as a musician in recent years have been my vocalizing of *Mureau* or my shouting of another text, *62 Mesosctics re Merce Cunningham.*

My first mesostic was written as prose to celebrate one of Edwin Denby's birthdays. The following ones, each letter of the name being on its own line, were written as poetry. *A given letter capitalized does not occur between it and the preceding capitalized letter.* I thought that I was writing acrostics, but Norman O. Brown pointed out that they could properly be called "mesostics" (row not down the edge but down the middle). Writing about Merce Cunningham for James Klosty's forthcoming book of photographs, I tried to write syntactically as I had in the case of the *Mesostics Re and Not Re Marcel Duchamp*, but the length of Cunningham's name proved to be an obstacle. I suddenly thought that length together with the name's being down the middle would turn from obstacle to utility if the letters were touching both vertically and horizontally. The poem would then have a spine and resemble Cunningham himself, the dancer. Though this is not the case ( these mesostics more resemble waterfalls or ideograms), this is how they came to be made. I used over seven hundred different type faces and sizes available in Letraset and, of course, subjected them to I Ching chance operations. No line has more than one word or syllable. Both syllables and words were obtained from Merce Cunningham's *Changes: Notes on Choreography* and from thirty-two other books most used Cunningham in relation to his work. The words were subjected to a process which brought about in some cases syllable exchange between two or more of them. This process produced new words not to be found in any dictionary but reminiscent of words everywhere to be found in James Joyce's *Finnegans Wake.*

Regarding *Finnegans Wake* I notice that though Joyce's subjects, verbs, and objects are unconventional, their relationships are the ordinary ones. With the exception of the Ten Thunderclaps and rumblings here and there, *Finnegans Wake* employs syntax. Syntax gives it a rigidity from which classical Chinese and Japanese were free. A poem by Bashō, for instance, floats in space: any English translation merely takes a snapshot of it; a second translation shows it in quite another light. Only the imagination of the reader limits the number of the poem's possible meanings.

Syntax, according to Norman O. Brown, is the arrangement of the army. As we move away from it, we demilitarize language. This demilitarization of language is conducted in many ways: a single language is pulverized; the boundaries between two or more languages are crossed; elements not strictly linguistic (graphic, musical) are introduced; etc. Translation becomes, if not impossible, unnecessary. Nonsense and silence are produced, familiar to lovers. We begin to actually live together, and the thought of separating doesn't enter our minds.

My work in this field is tardy. It follows the poetry of Jackson MacLow and Clark Coolidge, my analogous work in the field of music, and my first experiments (preceding *Mureau*, but likewise derived from Thoreau's *Journal*), texts for *Song Books (Solos for Voice 3-92)*, and *Solo for Voice 30*. Concrete and sound poets have also worked in this field for many years, though many, it seems to me, have substituted graphic or musical structures for syntactical ones, not having seen that man-made structures themselves (including structures in fields other than language: government in its nonutilitarian aspects, and zoos, for instance) must give way if those beings they were designed to control, whether people, animals, plants, sounds, or words, are to continue on earth to breathe and be.

I now write without syntax and sometimes with it.

In the fall of 1971 I received a letter from Norman O. Brown. He advised me to stop reading Jacques Ellul (at his advice I had been reading *The Technological Society*) and instead to read *The Chinese Road to Socialism* by E. L. Wheelwright and Bruce McFarlane. "What's happening in China is really important. China maybe has stepped into the future. Perhaps we have to acknowledge that (for our sins) America is no longer the future". My first thought was that Brown, too close to his university students, had received from them an interest in Mao that didn't belong to him.

When I returned from several bookstores with *The Chinese Road to Socialism* and an anthology of Mao's writings, I expected in reading them to find myself on the other side of the fence.

I knew it would be necessary to concentrate my attention on world improvement, to eliminate from my mind all thoughts about art. Contemporary Chinese arts are timely advertisements for the revolution, not significant expressions of it. Fortunately I had listened when Jasper Johns said, "I can imagine a society without any art at all, and it is not a bad society."

I was deeply touched in the Wheelwright and McFarlane book by the account of the material and spiritual changes in Chinese environment, technology, and society. I was immediately glad that seven hundred million people were no longer divided between what Fuller calls the haves and the have-nots. I was cheered by the news that one-fifth of the world's population were "fighting self-interest" and "serving the people." Just the news that people of all ages (the very young and the very old, and the usual able-bodied) were working together to turn desert into garden was refreshing: I had become numb from the social habit (practiced indiscriminately in the U.S.A., only politically in China) of getting rid of people, even killing them when feasible. I can't forget visits to my mother who lived the last years of her life unwillingly in a "comfortable" New Jersey nursing home. She begged to be taken home but her home no longer existed.

Wheelwrights and McFarlane's observations of changes in Chinese human nature were recently corroborated for me by Jumay Chu, a young American dancer who returned in the fall of '72 from a visit to China. Jumay told me she had asked a Chinese factory worker whether he was happy. (He was doing work to which he had been assigned that she herself wouldn't have enjoyed doing because it was repetitive and boring.) The factory worker didn't understand her question. He was doing his work as part of China's work; he was one person in the Chinese family.

In Mao's writing I skipped over the texts which are those of a general speaking to his soldiers, though I read carefully the rules he gave them regarding right conduct among persons of occupied land: to assist them with their work, to care for their well-being and property. "We Communists are like seeds and the people are like the soil. Wherever we go, we must unite with the people, take root and blossom among them." Though the history of the Chinese Revolution 'is a history of violence, it included the Long March, a grand retreat that reminds me of the Thoreau-influenced social actions of Gandhi, Martin Luther King, and the Danes in their response to Hitler's invasion.

I felt very close to Mao when I read in his biography that as a young man he had studied with great interest the texts of anarchism. And his admonitions to the people during the Chinese Cultural Revolution, including the very young, admonitions to revolt against authority, including his own authority, were ones with which I wholeheartedly concur. "It is right to rebel." "Bombard the headquarters."

Observed from a Western distance, Mao often seemed to be leading China into chaos. But it was to Chaos himself, in Kwang-tse's writings, that the Spirit of the Clouds put his questions when he felt the need to improve the world.

Throughout his thinking, I admired Mao's clear-headedness. He saw, for instance, that the solution of the Chinese problem was necessarily specifically Chinese. It would be wrong for it to be merely Russian. The largest number of Chinese people were peasants and the largest number of peasants were poor. The revolution in China was therefore to begin with them and in relation to their needs.

This looking to the masses made me think of Fuller, his vision of a world society in which all people, no matter their age, are properly students. The good life is a university different from those we now have, from which while living we never graduate. The World Revolution to come ("the greatest of them all"), apolitical, nonviolent, intelligent because comprehensively and regeneratively problem solving (cf. Mao: We must learn to look at problems all-sidedly, seeing the reverse as well as the obverse side of things) is a "Student Revolution."

I began then to search for the common denominator between Mao and Fuller, and, when I came across seemingly irreconcilable differences between the two, I decided to listen to both. For instance, Fuller's advice, "Don't change man; environment" and Mao's directive: "Remould people to their very souls; revolutionize their thinking."

Diasetz Suzuki often pointed out the Zen's nondualism arose in China as a result of problems encountered in translating India's Buddhist texts. Pali had syntax: Chinese did not. Indian words for concepts in opposition to one another did not exist in Chinese. *Fixity* became *mountain-mountain*; *flexibility* became *springweather-springweather*. Buddhism became Zen Buddhism. Looking for an Indian precedent, Chinese patriarchs chose the Flower Sermon of the Buddha, a sermon in which no word was spoken. Reading Mao's text *On Contradiction*, I think of it as a 20th century expression of nondualistic thought.

# CBC Interview re Bach
## with Anne Gibson

New York, November 1985

The following text is a typescript in proportional notation
of a recorded interview made in December 1984 in Toronto.
Each page has thirty-six lines, and takes 1½ minutes to
read. Every two lines take five seconds. Page six ends
with two blank lines, page 10 with four. Page 11 begins
with two blank lines and ends with one. Page 13 begins
with one blank line. Page 15 ends just before 3 blank lines.

*What I wondered was whether or not you would comment on*
*how you perceive the mind of*
*Bach*                       *whether you perceive it*
*as*                                 *uh . . . . .*
*. . . . . . . . . . . .*                  *a mind that was*
*capable of pure mathematics or a mind that*
*was tempered by emotions*
*do you see I think that it's*          *through*
*the music we get an idea of the mind*      *and*
*I wondered what yours was.*


                  I                 it seems
to me when I thi when I think of Bach I I'm not
so sure that I think of a mm           a
mind                  as much as uh
                                    uh
           as I think of a
                      a
       a person
whose life          was uh dedicated to music.
                       It it's quite
uh
                           I don't
I don't even know how          h
    how long his life was.
        But I uh        I do know that he
had many children, that many of them became
              uh          c       com-
posers, that he was         uh constantly
    uh writing music, because each uh
    each Sunday             must have
uhm

been the occasion for another first (laughs) performance.
And besides that        one hears of his visits
                                        to uh other mu-
sicians.                        In        And at
that time                        it wa it was not
easy to travel                        but I'v I'v
I've often thought of his        uh
leaving                        wherever he was
                        and going                uh
north                to                to visit Buxtehude.


                                H        h        he
        he . . . . . . . . uh                        must
                                w                with all
those children,                and with his admir-
ation for other musicians                and for his
own                        constant activity,
                        he must not have
taken any time to divide                himself into
                                                        on
the one hand a mind                and on the other
hand uh                uh emotions hmm?
He must have been all
        h        altogether                                uh
one person constantly active.
                                        *I think what*
                *uh . . . . . . ..*
                        *what it's hard t ah what I find hard*
*to have explained is what it is*
                        *in the conception of the music*
                                        *which seems*
*so mathematically intricate*
                (interrupting)        I I think mathematics is the
wrong word.
                        uhm

It h his                    his
ah Bach's music is characterized
I believe

                                                    by

                        uh . . . .
            starting with a rather simple
                        uh
        bu uh n simple's the wrong word uhw
uh starting with a short                        musical                                uh
                        motive.


And then                                            uh
        through repetition and variation
            to                    of that motive
                                            to
        bring
        a . . . .            piece of music into exist-
ence.


                                    *And*
        And uh        uh Schoenberg teaching us this
                            said uhm


when asked what variation was
            he said variation is also        repeti-
tion
                            with some things
changed
and some things not.


                            The uh
        other thing that characterizes uhm
                    Bach's music

                        is  that  if  you
                                    if  you  take  a
given  piece                and  you
look  at  it                    from  the  beginning  to  the  end
                you  see  that  there's  something  happen-
ing  at                       at  every
            smallest                    uh
                            division  point
                            so  that  the
        so  that  the  rhythm
                                is                  if  if  th
if  for  instance  there's  a  gap  in  one  line
                            or  a  long  note
                or  a  silence,
            the  other  lines  all  fill  it  up.
                        So  that  the  rhythm  is
is  constant                            and
mechanical.
I  mean  to  say  as  dependable  as  a  machine  hmm?
                        It's  un  it's  not  unpre-
dictable.  Once  it  starts  going,          it  continues  going  in  exactly  that  same  way  until  it's
(laughs)  finished.
                    *Now* . . . . . . . . . . . . . *if*  (interrupting)
    So  you  see  if                if  you're  going
to  make  a          a  machine  like  that
            which  isn't  going  to  stop  running  the
way  it  runs                          and  if
it's            uh        employing  a  motive
                which  it  is  using
            to  make  itself
            which              is  either  repeated
or  varied  and  if  the  variation  is  a  repetition,
        some  things  changed  and  some  things  not,
                uh                there  you  have

*it.*

*Now* (interrupting) And furthermore e i th it has
to be done before Sunday.
                    (laughs)

                                        *OK* You have a
deadline.  (laughs) *What is it*                    *that*
*makes this machine*
                    *capable*              *of astonishing some*
*listeners*                *spiritually?*


                                *e th* There're
so many possible answers to that question
                    that I don't know whether we
should even begin.              The
music is so often played in places where th they
are e b giving attention to spiritual matters.


                    So that              uh .
. . .      it i it does it for that reason.
        It's        it's the      it's the expected
                    sound              in the spiritual en-
vironment.              Hmm?


        y Or you could say t two plus two equals
four.              (laughs)
                                        *When it's*
                    *not*                *in a spiritual envi-*
*ronment?*                        Does it do it then?
                        *It has done.*
        OK.              Then then it has
        that's because of the action of memory.
                                        *Oh,*
                    *elaborate a bit on that.*
                    You remember having been
in church hearing it.              And now

you find yourself in the forest.
And someone happens to pass by with a radio
playing The Art of the Fugue. Hmm? (laughs)


                              *(laughs) You're saying it's not inherent
in the music.* No. It's a It's a qu                 uh
. . . .                  Do you Don't you know the
story of the                 man from Africa, black
     man who was                          taken
to a concert in London
                                   and
     afterwards                              uh the
music had gone from before Bach,
             included Bach, and went on to uh some
modern music.
     And they asked him afterwards what he
thought of the           of the music and he said
why did they play the same piece over and over
again? (laughs)
                                   *(laughs) OK.*
             *Then this*                      *the next
question that comes to my mind is*
                         *given what you've said*
                              Differe differ-
ent cultures have different memories. *Tha*
          *Bach's music has been elevated above and beyond other
Baroque music*                                  *by
us?*
*Is there an explanation for that within the music?*




                         I

I don't think anything has been
        uh . . . . . .
     p say         as        as your remark
                suggests I don't think
that anything has been permanently done
              to anything outside
of us                        to
put it        at        a     higher
   or     lower    point.
                      uh
     If if it has been done and if we think
it has been done           then
we're simply not making use
    of that          of that thing.
             Because our
      our way of using things
is           within us.
   Not outside of us.

          We h
e must          make
our own        uh . . . . . .
    experience.
   And th      one thing w
uh will   uh will g    uh
we will give our attention      to
one thing at one time and to another thing at
another time.     And I will
at least I      uh will not
automatically elevate
          something
      or or a whole body of
of work.    I remember   I m
       uh   loving
   Bach.

                        And a
at the time that I did
                    I
knew a           a very great musician
uh Richard Buhlig
who made an arrangement
of The Art of the Fugue of Bach
     for two pianos.
        And I                        had
the very great pleasure of hearing many performances of that Art of the Fugue in Southern California when Buhlig was alive


                    uh . . . .              I had
the feeling              something like what
you've                  expressed at that time
                    that uhm . . . .
     I needed no other
     uh music      really              than that
                        to hear.      I was
so deeply involved in it.
                    And I remember being
surprised                uh
     one day                        when
Buhlig said that uhm

                        that he hoped
he lived long enough              to play
Mozart.

                        And I said
what do you mean?
        Because       m      my mind at
that point             being absorbed with
Bach                   when it moved
over t        to those six          letters
        with a Z in it
                    uh . . . .      felt

itself to be in a field of frivolity          hmm?
                                                  I said
what do you mean? And                    he went
on I forget what he said I was so astonished
                          but                    e he
s       he went on to say that uh . . . .
              Bach was all good and well   (laughs)
                                        but the great
musician was Mozart.

*Do you recall*
     *what it was about* And that he wanted to end
his days      playing Mozart.          But that
he thought it would be too difficult.


              *Do you recall what it was about Bach that absorbed*
*you at the time?* a All those things that I've just
been talking about.                    And
                    later fortunately I had the
                                        I had
two experiences: one of listening to Mozart
                                                  and
another time          uhm . . . .                oh
kind of          a       study of Mozart
                          that led me to
a view of music that was different
                                  uh than the view
that        that the music of Bach gave.

    uh . . . .      The difference is the difference
between everything fitting together
as it does in Bach hmm?
and coming out to                    to reassure us
about                    the . . . .      existence of
order. Hmm?


65

uh . . . .                          It
m Mozart does another thing.
He            he . . . . . . uh
provides  us  with  a  m
with a music which is characterized by multiplicity.                          Not characterized  by  unity.                          But
multiplicity.                          And .
. . .      uh . . . .                          you have
the feeling that if there were something
            if he had been able to give us
                          some other thing
            than  he  did                          in <u>Don</u>
<u>Giovanni</u>                          that he would
have  willingly  given  it.

                                    That th
that he left the doors open
                          to                   to X
                          to the
            unknown and the excitement
                          and the . . . . uh . . . .
            affirmation  of  life,
                          rather than the affirm-
ation  of  order        hmm?


            is                   what I love
      in Mozart.

                                    *Then this*
*will  seem  an  odd  question, perhaps, but maybe it's not*
                                    *but        I am*
*curious  to  know  if  there  is  any  kinship  between  you  as  a*
*composer*                          *and the composer Bach.*

My relation to                    to
to uh . . . .
Bach is through my        teachers.

And                              I've already
mentioned them.        One was Richard Buhlig
            and the other was uh
        Schoenberg.


And that's a kind of kinship.


                            uhm . . . .
    Schoenberg


    used to speak of the uhm . . . .
                structural importance of
harmony.
    And I think he saw music
                as a
                primarily


    a concern for uh
pitch relationships.


                            My
        my uh . . . . . .


    experience involved uhm . . . .

at one point
a remark from the filmmaker Oscar Fischin-
ger                              and he said everything                     in . . . . uhm
. . . .          creation has a spirit and the
the spirit of a . . . . m
                    a                    e
that spirit can be released
by it's being set into vibration.

uh That remark so inspired me that I went
around                 hitting everything and
touching everything and rubbing everything to
hear    what                     sound
          could be produced.
          And so I entered into the world
of noise                                    that
uhm . . . .          Varese had opened
                    and that
e much uh . . . .                              what
we now call world music has
has been in.

                              uh What I took
then from                 from uhm

I'm    speaking    of    kinship    now    n
          what I took then from my
     from the teaching that          that
Schoenberg gave me was not
     harmony itself
but                 the function that harmony
     was playing which was          he said
structural                 and I looked for
                    a structure that would
be hospitable to noises.

Because I knew that har-
mony wouldn't be.

And I found just
empty time.

*It seems like kinship*
*is simply the open house*                    *for* The
structure.    The . . . .            the
perhaps then we come to the uhm

and that structure now in my
work has uhm . . . .
given way to process,
just as a table would give
way to the      to the weather. Hmm?

So that uh .
. . . . .

I I don't know what the kinship is

except
through uhm . . . . .

Well                              I'v
I'm afraid w
we have to uhm . . . . side with
Mozart                              and his
uh                    and
at least Mozart as I see him uh
. . . . . . . someone concerned with mutiplicity

69

at that point                                        uh .
. . .                    we we're glad to have Bach
                              too.

              (laughs)                        *Can you*
         *explain there is a renaissance amongst perfor-*
*mers* Mmhmm *And most audiences*
      *from*                *all kinds of walks of life*
                                 *for the music of Bach.*
      *We see it clearly.*         *Now more than ever.*
                            *Have you an explanation for*
*that?*


                                           *Why they*
*want to go back to*                             *that*
*voice of the 18th century.*




                              I
                I think it has to do with
    the uh                    paying attention to
              or                  order
                              and unity.


                                 *And so we*
*miss our t s so*
         *there's a general* (Interrupting) But I don't
    I don't think it's uhm . . . . .
                   I think it's a little bit look-
ing out the back window
            rather than moving ahead as Marshall
McLuhan would                        would uh .
    .                       say we
                              whether we want


                              70

to or not, we are            we are going
forward         hmm?
                    And that for-
wardness is definitely electronic.

    And uhm . . . .              the
Bach          uh        the
the sound of Bach and everything doesn't have
to do with electronics. It has to do with machinery.
             A machine that works quite
well.
                       But
it      evide     But it doesn't have those mysterious      uhm . . . . . .
    uh presences of         unpredictability

             in it that it that are
a almost the hallmark of uhm . . . .
    of electronics.
           We have as McLuhan said
extended the central nervous system.
    And we're in a world where anything can
happen.          And that's not the
world Bach was in.
        So
that if there is this general having-recourse--
to-Bach,         it is a retreat
                 from
      uh     a situation that the
people are actually in      and that
sooner or later      they will
have to enjoy. (laughs)

Kenneth Gaburo

KENNETH GABURO was born in 1926, in Raritan, New Jersey. He is internationally recognized for his innovative work as composer, writer, teacher, performer, publisher. His writings include experimental compositions (opera, songs, chamber, choral, tape, computer, video, film, stage, music-theater, text-sound, orchestra), short stories, poetry, and philosophical, aesthetic, technical essays.

Gaburo is founder of the highly acclaimed New Music Choral Ensemble which was created in 1960. Its repertory has ranged from complex twentieth century choral music to theater works such as those by Beckett, Albee, and Brün. In 1974 Gaburo founded Lingua Press which has published 115 works to date by 71 authors. Its issuances, generally on the "cutting edge" of new thought and practice, cover a variety of fields in the Arts, Humanities, and Sciences.

Many works of Kenneth Gaburo have been recorded (Columbia, Nonesuch, MGM-Heliodore, CRI Orion, Ars Nova), and numerous references to his work may be found including Salzman: *20th Century Music*; *Who's Who*; Reimann *Musik Lexikon*; Grove's *Dictionary of Music and Musicians*; Ewen's *Comprehensive Biographical Dictionary of American Composers*; *Perspectives of New Music* (an entire issue). His honors include awards from the Guggenheim, UNESCO, Thorne, Fromm, Rockefeller, and Koussevitzky Foundations, and grants for linguistic research from the University of Illinois and California Research Boards.

In 1980, Gaburo staged the first uhrtext production of Partch's *Bewitched* for the Berlin Festival, and in 1982 began his third massive theater, THE SCRATCH PROJECT: ACTS (Testimony, Antiphony VIII-Revolution, Pentagon/y, and De/bate). Recently he has been in residence at Mills College (Milhaud Chair), and is currently director of the Experimental Music Studio at the University of Iowa. Previously he has taught at the University of California-San Diego, the University of Illinois.

**Rethink:**

Kenneth Gaburo

It is particularly difficult for me to speak about a work of mine once it is made. No matter the form of presentation with respect to some prime referent, (in this case, the actual Minim-Tellig videotape), something is always missed; perhaps something crucial to the sense of the work which I would like a reader to know, but which might not be self-evident. At least I have the uneasy feeling that this is so.

Now, of course, one can always say something in any recursion; for instance, provide some parataxis, as in the following excerpt of a 'manifesto', (+ comments), to myself **dated 5.12.72**:

1. "Minim-Tellig: (a) interactive working out of performance dimensions; (b) reel-reel state-of-the-art technology, (no apology); (c) camera does not bias; performers do; (d) video apparatus as a performing instrument; (e) minim is not to be some videotaping of a live performance, (i.e., not some document), but an intrinsic work with video; (f) screen dimension is not to be an extension of the cathod-ray tube, but an intimate stage; (kgnb: a stage, say, really for one viewer-performer at a time; an audience of a million is not the same as an audience of one, of a million such; I am not into filling houses; there are not a million people in my, or any other, living room; this notion has to make a significant difference in the kind of work minim-tellig becomes); (g) in any video take which could become the master, the camera is fixed; (cf. same technique as for Give-Take); (h) editing is censorship; keep it to a minimum; (kgnb: preferably use only continuous real-time takes; true, the videotape is to be made from a so-called real-time live performance; but minim's essential being, ---as entity---is video; it's to be as-if the live "performance" aspect, ---necessary to generate the tape---, will become, in itself, an idea; a subtext; perhaps a phantom; what is to be viewed on tape should not easily be observable elsewhere, ---e.g., a live performance---, without doing violence to

75

minim's nature; after the fact, the studio performance could be said to have mimicked the videotape; hmm, not bad; the other is no longer to be found, although someone might want to make another videotape from the 'score', sometime) (i) the tape is not to be of an event which was, but one which is; where it is in the set; on the tape; (j) except for obvious techniques which could distinguish minim from what some future technology might do with it, there is to be no sense of date; (kgnb: the issue of ecological deterioration through human abuse will be around for some time; ecology is not-yet cliche', nor is political art; although I suspect antagonists will soon want to have them so)."

2.    "Intelligibility, (+ Minimal): (a) derive aspects of minim's concept from information and communication theories, speech synthesis, and my psychoacoustic research; (b) work with channel noise, signal loss, (e.g., masking), actual and as metaphor; (kgnb: this would not be to make minim intentionally obscure, but only to emphasize the implicit obscurity in language when it *appears* to be clear!); (c) consider perceptual noise of the viewer, performer, composer; (d) isn't intelligibility curiously interwoven with cliche'?; (kgnb: think about this); (e) free up text transforms from their quantized, statistical, informational basis; (f) develop the acoustical, physiological, syntactical aspects of language; (kgnb: non-semantic, pero'; this could generate the multi-level theatre I want); (g) perhaps minim should be a dance?; (h) work toward a whole view of language; (kgnb: the expression "para-language", ---i.e., "noise" in linguistic terms, seems to me to be merely a temporarily unresolved condition of language, generally; and of music)."

But, beyond levels of mere or elaborate information, what of a more substantive nature can be said?

Actually, the difficulty I have with 'speaker' about a work of mine once it is made is not connected to "speaking" as it is usually understood, but with the actual *forms* of speaking, (e.g., text, video), and its materials, (e.g., paper, tape), and its time-space, (e.g., when-where), with respect to some referent.

As I view this text, (being made now), in the light of the accompanying graphic, (made several months ago), each in the light of the original videotape, (made 14 years ago), a continuing agony is triggered; an agony which, in this particular circumstance, is: *the text is not the graphic is not the videotape.* This "noise" raises the matter of intelligibility to a level not at all considered at the time: at this point in the writing of *this* text, I confess I don't know whether I can, (or will have) put my speaking in any frame which could suggest a predictable familiarity with the videotape, if-when seen. And yet, it is often assumed that matters such as this text or graphic can actually *represent* some referent to which each presumably refers. My difficulty here is further complicated by the fact that the compositional *impulse* for minim, which influenced me then, is adumbrated beyond recall. Now, it is this impulse, and its *sense* to me, which cannot be given here with any surety; and, it is also this sense that I would most like the reader to know something of.

But surely, there was one. Without some extraordinarily seductive impulse, I cannot imagine how minim, ---which involved three dedicated, untiring performers, and took nine months to make---, could have been accomplished, or why, otherwise, it would have been of interest to pursue. Certainly I care about minim, still. And the knowledge of having composed it is persistently beautiful. But I cannot remember what minim's impulse was, or what I loved about it. However, without some 'propulsive' like-kind of fuel, it is not possible for me to recapture the sense of minim in a new form, either.

Maybe I make too much of this desire to shed some light. But, in a way, by not pushing for it, I am left mutus-elinguis, ---(speechless, dumb)---; in a way, ex-lingua, ---(without elegance) ---; in a way, merely doing not much of anything but loquitor-ari, ---(chattering)---.

(So push)!

From the time of minim's completion, I can say there has been a strange sort of *forgetting* going on. This is not altogether due to some decompositional process, ---(which I always do anyway, before beginning a new work. It is intentional. It is for forgetting. It is for clearing the slate, ---impulses having been purged. It is for emptying myself with regard to that work. It is over. This task is especially important. I know that the intensity of my experience, if allowed to continue, ((and, thereby, to unduly "get off" on it)), could provoke a continuous succession of like-works. After all, no work exhausts its possible implications; so why not go on with it, ad nauseam? But I am not interested in that, either. Composition of the kind I refer to is for forgetting impulse)---; or ageing.

To say I would do minim differently now, ---even assuming the same impulse---, is only to be reminded of how fragile, original choices are. In no sense can they be regarded as absolute. At best, I see minim as having come from some self, which I am no longer. To compose is always to compose one's self from where one is at that time. Self is also fragile.

Could it be that it is this 'forgetting' of a former self which makes composition so desireable, and, at times of desired recursions, such as this one, so agonizing? (My parents must have been driven quite nuts with this. As soon as they thought they had a handle on what it was I was say-doing, I was say-doing something else).

Could it be that it is my curiosity for 'dark alleys' which leads me to suppose that impulses lurk there? (But any dark alley which interests me, simply appears. I am never prepared. And, when impulses do come, they have no name).

Could it be that compositions begin by accident; perhaps remain so in the light of experience and forgetting? (Now this is a very high praise I give myself, for the immensity of the compositional act does not at all suggest mandatory, intense, preparation, or eternal retention. And yet, somehow a 'right' composition, ---the 'needed' one---, here and now, then and there, is always evoked). But this composition is not the only possible one, and, yes, *is* the only possible one it could be for the moment.

(These matters are not paradoxical)!

Each time this situation obtains I feel like a radical. Knowing this has led me to deny the usual, current, ubiquitous cliches' of "avantgarde", "experimental", "far-out", "strange", + "whatever". In this age of 'superfly', such 'expressive' claims are not strong enough to characterize certain kinds of work. Radical is; radical accident is.

Yes: sometimes by process (es), but not in material; sometimes in material and not by process (es); sometimes by both; sometimes by neither. Curiously, it is the latter possibility which, now and then, seems the most radical to me. When certain radical-accidental process(es) and material(s) are absent, (e.g. such as a gymnist's mat used percussively by five dancer-acrobats who fall in and out of each other, on it, incessantly, for 25 minutes in this writer's *My, My, My, --- What A Wonderful Fall*), I am particularly vulnerable to some life-experience which simply, 'seems'; (cf. the

78

short story in my collection, *Serious Music-Making In San Diego, And Other Happy Memories*, which begins: *My Grandmother was a Flower*).

Now, it is true that *traces* of the videotape may be found herein, (e.g., the graphic stills of Lin have not been cropped; the images fill the video screen as shown). But, since tape is not text is not graphic, the contents, herein, each in its own way, do as much to establish their own identity as they do to elaborate, and, (at the same time), to contradict minim's videotape. Perhaps speaking should be left at this. Afterall, there is this cliche' about "let the music speak for itself", or, this one: "if music needed words, I would have said it with words and not with music".

But no: 'no more say' is not an ending; and yes: the pretense that any form of 'speaking' can be expected to represent its referent as well as it represents itself is a socio-political conceptual dysfunction, and needs some resolution.

No, it is not that these words and graphics are insufficient to convey some sense of the minim videotape; nor are they incapable of expressing some quite intimate matters imbedded therein. But, yes: in this case it is the very nature of paper, itself, which causes the agony.

No matter this graphic's exotic (I think) impressions (imprints), herein minim resides in a silent, frozen world. This world renders unintelligible, the crucial time-space factors on which the 'noisy' videotape depends: movement, light, play, sound, fluid sculpture; physicality; et alia, et alia.

But, as I stare at these photographic stills, taken of particular videotape frames, an overpowering sense begins to come over me. I am only now becoming conscious of the fact that these particular stills exaggerate something of the 'non-frozen' *isolation* of the videotape; and stir up a feeling I have/had every time I see/saw a dozer. I am enabled by an intense sense of some momentary relief from my agony.

This text, and graphic do not represent the videotape. They only merely *refer* to it. Now I know I have been dickeying around with this notion all along, but it only became clear once the stills got to me in the way I have said. Because of this disassociation among forms I am hearing, it is also becoming clear that in their seeming paradoxical states, resides an expressive, metaphoric, bonding.

Perhaps *isolation* was the sensual impulse which precipitated minim so long ago. Certainly it is not something one can, or needs to prove. I simply don't remember. But now, here and now, as I face these stills, and as I experience the feelings they evoke, I can imagine it. There is a strangely wonderful resonance going on.  At the least, isolation is surely the impulse that seduced me into making sense of what I've done herein.

(1.5.87, Iowa City)

SHOW

TELLIES:

# VIDEO
# COMPOSITIONS

GIVE-TAKE

MINIM-TELLIG ONE,
TWO,
THREE,

1973

# KENNETH GABURO                    1973

---AND SO I WAS TALKING TO LIN ABOUT HER SHAPING
OF MY MINIM-THREE ONE DAY AS WE VIEWED THE VIDEO
TAKES IN THE SENSE THAT IT NOW NEEDED A FINAL TW
IST SOME PARTICULAR EXPRESSIVE FOCUS SINCE THE O
RIGINAL TEXT (LONDON BRIDGES) HAD BEEN DECOMPOSE
D BY CERTAIN LINGUISTIC TRICKS IN ORDER TO REVEA
L AN 'ANTI-DEVELOPER' SUB-TEXT (e.g.,    -UNDONE
-RIDGES) AND HOW ALL OF THAT DOZING REALLY  MADE
ME NERVOUS AND THAT OTHERWISE HER TRANSFORMATION
S AND ARTICULATIONS WERE NOW SO BEAUTIFUL AND IT
WAS TRUE WE HAD ACCOMPLISHED THE TASK OF COMPOSI
NG WITH VIDEO MAKING THREE A REALITY THERE IN TH
E SET AND NOT A REPRESENTATION OF ONE  AND AFTER
LISTENING TO ME GO ON LIKE THIS FOR SOME TIME LI
N WITH REMARKABLE SIMPLICITY SAID  DO YOU MEAN I
SHOULD TRY TO PERFORM IT NERVOUSLY ?  I SAID WHY
NOT ? SHE SAID I'LL TRY AND SOME DAYS LATER SAID
PERFORMING THREE NERVOUSLY MAKES ME TWITCH AND I
SAID NERVOUS FOR ME TWITCH FOR YOU  A GRAND FINE
TUNING VERY INCISIVE  GO FOR IT  WHEN PEOPLE SEE
THREE THEY ALMOST ALWAYS NOTICE        (composer's
workbook entry retyped 3.15.86    entered 3.4.73)

1
2
3

© LINGUA PRESS 1976

# 9 MINIM-TELLIG ONE [1]   [composition in 'knowns']                        1973

*for 1 performer at a time*

For the below-given text:

A. Select one general mode of transmission [e.g., declamatory].     This
   mode is to be held *constant* for all substitutions specified.

B. Select one general phrase characteristic [e.g., legato].     This
   characteristic is to be held *constant* for all substitutions specified.

C. Preserve the metrical schema     [i.e., as it would commonly be read ].
   This schema is to be held *constant* for all substitutions specified [2] .

D. 1]   for every phoneme [P], substitute phoneme [d] [3]
   2]   for every article [a], substitute a hand clap
   3]   for every preposition [of], substitute a finger snap
   4]   for every [;], substitute an ingressive whistle
   5]   for every [.], substitute a palatal tongue-click [forte]
   6]   for every [?], substitute a facial grimace
   7]   for every [,], substitute phoneme [n]; [long nasal tone]
   8]   for every past tense unit [-led; -ed], substitute silence
   9]   for every article [the], substitute some multiphonic
   10]  for every phonetic unit [-ers], cross/uncross legs [or
        some other appropriate contextual gesture]

[TEXT] [4]


        Peter Piper picked a peck of pickled peppers;
        A peck of pickled peppers Peter Piper picked.
        If Peter Piper picked a peck of pickled peppers,
        Where's the peck of pickled peppers Peter Piper picked? [5]

# FootNote for 9

**9**     MINIM-TELLIG ONE      [composition in 'knowns']

[1]     MINIM-TELLIG= minimal intelligibility

[2]     Substitution [D.7] is the only exception to this instruction. It is noted as a fermata in the coded text given below [fn.4].

[3]     Substitutions may be practiced separately or in combination. Ultimately, the task is to integrate the entire collection of substitutions into what remains of the original ordered text. The so-transformed text= a performable composition.

[4]     The textual transform, in coded and ordered array, is as follows [numbers refer to substitution numbers]:

> [1]eter [1]i[1]er [1]ick[8] [2] [1]eck [3] [1]ick[8] [1]e[1][10][4]
>
> [2] [1]eck [3] [1]ick[8] [1]e[1][10] [1]eter [1]i[1]er [1]ick[8][5]
>
> If [1]eter [1]i[1]er [1]ick[8] [2] [1]eck [3] [1]ick[8] [1]e[1][10][7]
>
> Where's [9] [1]eck [3] [1]ick[8] [1]e[1][10] [1]eter [1]i[1]er [1]ick[8][6]

[5]     A video composition of Minim-Tellig One, Two, Three is available from Lingua Press. The following is an extraction from a detailed description of the video composition:

    ---"On the other hand, Minim-Tellig One, Two, Three require prolonged compositional deliberations, and therefore, deep analysis before, during, and after a particular concretion. In this case, a collection of nursery rhymes are treated as generative grammars. A first-level (?) transform of these grammars obtains by compositionally substituting certain discrete linguistic units for certain ones which appear in the original texts [while at the same time keeping certain textual properties invarient]. A second-level transform obtains by way of specific

and precise performer articulation. Keeping the first and second-level transforms constant, a third-level transform obtains by changing only the physiological attitude [environment, context] of each performer as each text is repeated. The genesis for this work was the following question:

What is constituted by the expression:
*Minimal Intelligibility?*"

*for 1 performer at a time*

A. Select one general mode of transmission [e.g., declamatory].     This mode is to be held *constant* for all substitutions specified.

B. Select one general phrase characteristic [e.g., legato].     This characteristic is to be held *constant* for all substitutions specified.

C. Preserve the metrical schema     [i.e., as it would commonly be read [2]]. This schema is to be held *constant* for all substitutions specified [2] .

D. 1] for every word [house] substitute word unit [zing] [3]
   2] for every word [the] substitute: right hand slap on thigh;intersect left hand slap on some resonant part of chair[4] with word following [the]
   3] for every word [built] substitute: ingressive/glottal ['ill'] as a multiphonic; minimize phoneme [l]; simultaneously cover both   eyes with finger tips.
   4] for every [.] substitute phoneme [t—$\dot{\text{i}}$]; simultaneously cross arms.
   5] for every [th] of this/that, simply *drop* the [th] element, relaxing from previous gesture as well. Also: simply *drop* the [l] of [lay], and the [J] of [Jack].
   6] for every word [malt] substitute the word [chaw] percussively.
   7] for every word [rat]  substitute [s$\Longleftarrow\dot{\text{i}}$] very high and very short .
   8] for every word [cat]  substitute fricative [f$\Longrightarrow\dot{\text{i}}$].
   9] for every word [worried] *freeze* in your position at the moment, and sing a very high note on phoneme [i].
   10] for every word [dog]  substitute silence.

[TEXT] [5]              This is the house that Jack built.
                        This is the malt
                        That lay in the house that Jack built.
                        This is the rat
                        That ate the malt
                        That lay in the house that Jack built.
                        This is the cat
                        That killed the rat
                        That ate the malt
                        That lay in the house that Jack built.
                        This is the dog
                        That worried the cat
                        That killed the rat
                        That ate the malt
                        That lay in the house that Jack built. 6

86

# FOOTNOTE FOR 10

**10** MINIM-TELLIG TWO     [composition in 'knowns']

[1]   cf. Minim-Tellig One, [fn.1]

[2]   Substitution [9] is the only exception to this instruction. It is noted as a fermata in the coded text given below [fn. 5 ]

[3]   cf. Minim-Tellig One, [fn.3]

[4]   Or some other appropriate instrument.

[5]   The textual transform in coded and ordered array, is as follows [numbers refer to substitution numbers]:

[5]is is [2] [1] [5]at [5]ack [3] [4]

[5]is [2] [6]

[5]at [5]ay in [2] [1] [5]at [5]ack [3] [4]

[5]is is [2] [7]

[5]at ate [2] [6]

[5]at [5]ay in [2] [1] [5]at [5]ack [3] [4]

[5]is is [2] [8]

[5]at killed [2] [7]

[5]at ate [2] [6]

[5]at [5]ay in [2] [1] [5]at [5]ack [3] [4]

[5]is is [2] [10]

[5]at [9] [2] [8]

[5]at killed [2] [7]

[5]at ate [2] [6]

[5]at [5]ay in [2] [1] [5]at [5]ack [3] [4]

[6]   Cf. Minim-Tellig One, [fn.5]

# 11

*for 1 performer at a time*

For the below-given text:

A. Select one general mode of transmission [e.g., declamatory].      This
   mode is to be held *constant* for all substitutions specified.

B. Select one general phrase characteristic [e.g., legato].      This
   characteristic is to be held *constant* for all substitutions specified.

C. Preserve the metrical schema    [i.e., as it would commonly be read ].
   This schema is to be held *constant* for all substitutions specified [2].

D. 1] for every phoneme [B,b] substitute a silently formed,   *but visible*
      [B,b]. Exception: the [b] in [tumble]
   2] for every *first* and *third* [,] in each stanza, substitute  the  word
      [see]. Treat [see] as an appoggiatura to  the  word which  follows.
   3] for every *second* [,] in each stanza, substitute the word     [saw].
      Treat [saw] as a 'glide' into the word which follows.
   4] for every *fourth* [,] in each stanza, substitute the word     [saw].
      Treat [saw] as a period [.]; follow [saw] with a kissing 'lip-
      smack'; treat the lip-smack as an appoggiatura into word [My].
   5] for every [.] in each stanza, substitute the word [so]. Treat [so]
      as a *transition* to the next stanza.
   6] for every word [my] stretch [hum into] the [m] slightly.
   7] for every phrase [fair lady] substitute a formant glide ad libitum.
      Include in this glide the central phonemes of [fair] and [lady].
   8] for every [need] of [need/les] substitute phoneme [i].
   9] for every [-les] of [need/les] substitute a gesture of your choice.
   10] for every [r] of [r/ust] substitute phoneme [L].

E. However, due to the number of substitutions desired,      a first level
   transform of the basic text was made. The substitutions given refer to
   the transformed text, and *not* to the basic text. In every other respect
   the directions A-D apply  as one performs the transformed text:

basic text:

text transform [3]:

**CONT'D**

MINIM-TELLIG THREE

11

basic text:

London Bridge is falling down,
falling down, falling down,
London Bridge is falling down,
My fair lady.

Build it up with iron bars,
iron bars, iron bars,
Build it up with iron bars,
My fair lady.

Iron bars will bend and break,
bend and break, bend and break,
Iron bars will bend and break,
My fair lady.

Build it up with needles and pins,
needles and pins, needles and pins,
Build it up with needles and pins,
My fair lady.

Pins and needles rust and bend,
rust and bend, rust and bend,
Pins and needles rust and bend,
My fair lady.

Build it up with penny loaves,
penny loaves, penny loaves,
Build it up with penny loaves,
My fair lady.

Penny loaves will tumble down,
tumble down, tumble down,
Penny loaves will tumble down,
My fair lady.

Build it up with gold and silver,
gold and silver, gold and silver,
Build it up with gold and silver,
My fair lady.

Gold and silver I've not got,
I've not got, I've not got,
Gold and silver I've not got,
My fair lady.

text transform [3]:

Un-done bridge is [ɔ][4] and [aʊ],
[ɔ] and [aʊ], [ɔ] and [aʊ],
Un-done bridge is [ɔ]  and [aʊ],
My fair lady.

Build'er up needs [aɪ ] and [aʳ],
[aɪ ] and [aʳ], [aɪ ] and [aʳ],
Build'er up needs [aɪ ] and [aʳ],
My fair lady.

[aɪ ] and [aʳ] can bend the [e],
bend the [ e], [ ɛ] the [e],
[aɪ] and [aʳ] can bend the [e],
My fair lady.

Build'er up needs needles and [ɪ],
needles and [ɪ], needles and [ɪ],
Build'er up needs needles and [ɪ],
My fair lady.

[ɪ] and needles can rust the [ɛ],
rust the [ɛ], rust the [ɛ],
[ɪ] and needles can rust the [ɛ],
My fair lady.

Build'er up needs [ɛ] and [o],
[ɛ] and [o], [ɛ] and [o],
Build'er up needs [ɛ] and [o],
My fair lady.

[ɛ] and [o] can tumble [aʊ],
tumble [aʊ], tumble [ aʊ],
[ɛ] and [o] can tumble [aʊ],
My fair lady.

Build'er up needs [o] and [ɪ],
[o] and [ɪ], [o] and [ɪ],
Build'er up needs [o] and [ɪ],
My fair lady.

[o] and [ɪ] can-trive [a] [ha],
-trive [a] [ha], -trive [a] [ha],
[o] and [ɪ] can-trive [a] [ha],
My fair lady. 5

89

# 11 MINIM-TELLIG THREE  [composition in 'knowns']

[1]     cf. Minim-Tellig One, [fn.1]

[2]     Substitution [7], and to a lesser degree substitution [6] are the two exceptions to this instruction. Substitution [7] is noted as a fermata in the coded text below.

[3]     cf. Minim-Tellig One, [fn.3]

[4]     Phonemic substitutions in this transform correspond to a *central* resonant phoneme for each corresponding word in the basic text. For example in line 1:
        falling  f[ɔ]lling;  down    d[aʊ]wn; etc. Structurally, such substitutions may be regarded as *proper nouns*. The textual transform in coded and ordered array, is as follows, [numbers refer to substitution numbers]:

[stanzas 1-5]

Un-done [1]ridge is [ɔ] and [aʊ][2]
[ɔ] and [aʊ][3] [ɔ] and [aʊ][2]
Un-done [1]ridge is [ɔ] and [aʊ][4]
[6]y [7]----------[5]

[1]uild'er up needs [aɪ] and [ɑʳ][2]
[aɪ] and [ɑʳ][3] [aɪ] and [ɑʳ][2]
[1]uild'er up needs [aɪ] and [ɑʳ][4]
[6]y [7]----------[5]

[aɪ] and [ɑʳ] can [1]end the [e][2]
[1]end the [e][3] [1][ɛ] the [e][2]
[aɪ] and [ɑʳ] can [1]end the [e][4]
[6]y [7]----------[5]

[1]uild'er up needs [8][9] and [ɪ][2]
[8][9] and [ɪ][3] [8][9] and [ɪ][2]
[1]uild'er up needs [8][9] and [ɪ][4]
[6]y [7]----------[5]

[ɪ] and [8][9] can [10]ust the [ɛ][2]
[10]ust the [ɛ][3] [10]ust the [ɛ][2]
[ɪ] and [8][9] can [10]ust the [ɛ][4]
[6]y [7]----------[5]

[5]     cf. Minim-Tellig One, [fn.5]

[stanzas 6-9]

[1]uild'er up needs [ɛ] and [o][2]
[ɛ] and [o][3] [ɛ] and [o][2]
[1]uild'er up needs [ɛ] and [o][4]
[6]y [7]----------[5]

[ɛ] and [o] can tumble [aʊ][2]
tumble [aʊ][3] tumble [aʊ][2]
[ɛ] and [o] can tumble [aʊ][4]
[6]y [7]----------[5]

[1]uild'er up needs [o] and [ɪ][2]
[o] and [ɪ][3] [o] and [ɪ][2]
[1]uild'er up needs [o] and [ɪ][4]
[6]y [7]----------[5]

[o] and [ɪ] can-trive [ɑ] [hɑ][2]
'trive [ɑ] [hɑ][3] 'trive [ɑ] [hɑ][2]
[o] and [ɪ] can-trive [ɑ] [hɑ][4]
[6]y [7]----------[5]

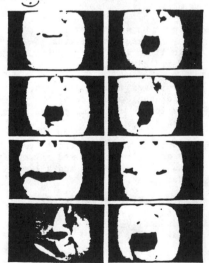

FOOTNOTE FOR 11

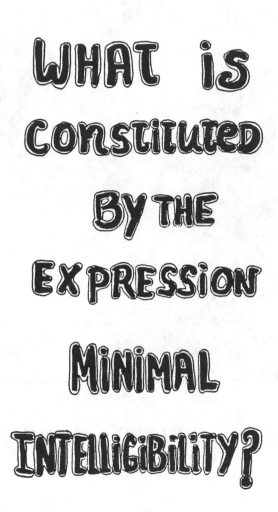

# WHAT is CONSTITUTED BY THE EXPRESSION MINIMAL INTELLIGIBILITY?

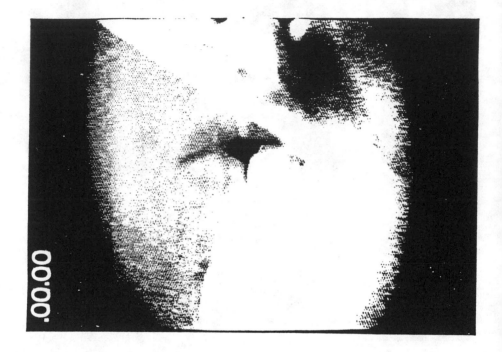

00.00

Un-done [1]ridge is [ɔ] and [ɑʊ][2]
[ɔ] and [ɑʊ][3] [ɔ] and [ɑʊ][2]
Un-done [1]ridge is [ɔ] and [ɑʊ][4]
[6]y [7]----------[5]

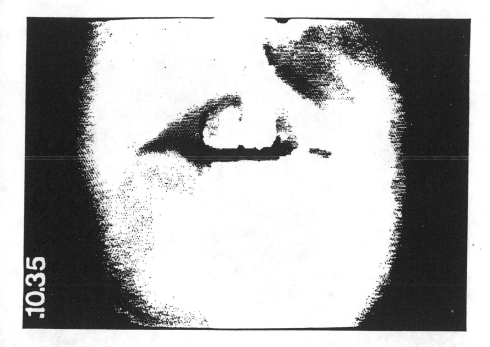

[1]uild'er up needs [aɪ] and [ɑʳ][2]
[aɪ] and [ɑʳ][3] [aɪ] and [ɑʳ][2]
[1]uild'er up needs [aɪ] and [ɑʳ][4]
[6]y [7]-----------[5]

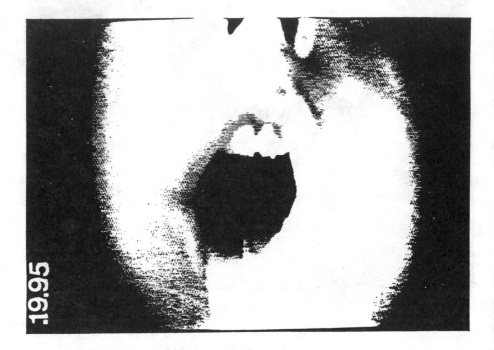

[aɪ] and [aʳ] can [1]end the [e][2]
[1]end the [e][3] [1][ɛ] the [e][2]
[aɪ] and [a̤ʳ] can [1]end the [e][4]
[6]y [7]----------[5]

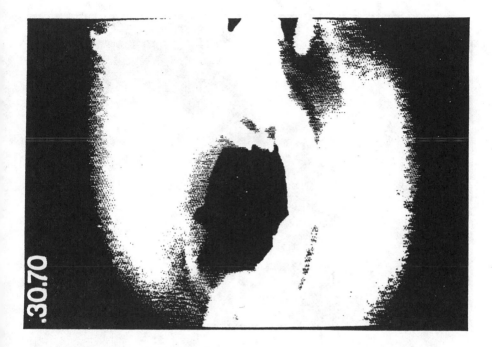

.30.70

[1]uild'er up needs [8][9] and [ɪ][2]
[8][9] and [ɪ][3] [8][9] and [ɪ][2]
[1]uild'er up needs [8][9] and [ɪ][4]
[6]y [7]----------[5]

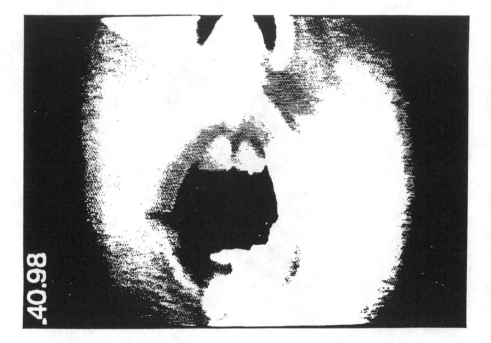

[ɪ] and [8][9] can [10]ust the [ɛ][2]
[10]ust the [ɛ][3] [10]ust the [ɛ][2]
[ɪ] and [8][9] can [10]ust the [ɛ][4]
[6]y [7]----------[5]

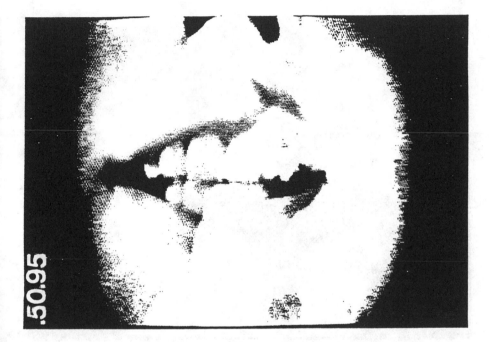

[1]uild'er up needs [ɛ] and [ɔ][2]
[ɛ] and [ɔ][3] [ɛ] and [ɔ][2]
[1]uild'er up needs [ɛ] and [ɔ][4]
[6]y [7]-----------[5]

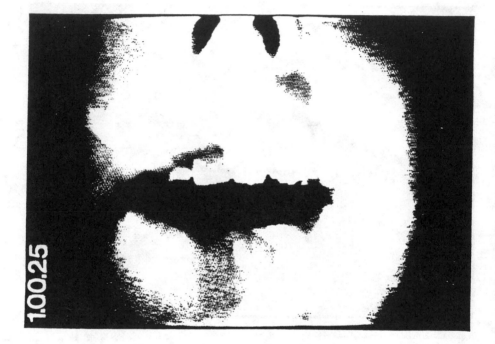

[ɛ] and [ɔ] can tumble [aʊ] [2]
tumble [aʊ] [3] tumble [aʊ] [2]
[ɛ] and [ɔ] can tumble [aʊ] [4]
[6] y [7] ------------ [5]

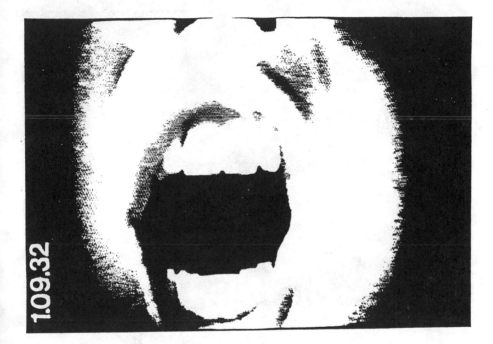

[1]uild'er up needs [ɔ] and [ɪ][2]
[o] and [ɪ][3] [o] and [ɪ][2]
[1]uild'er up needs [o] and [ɪ][4]
[6]y [7]-----------[5]

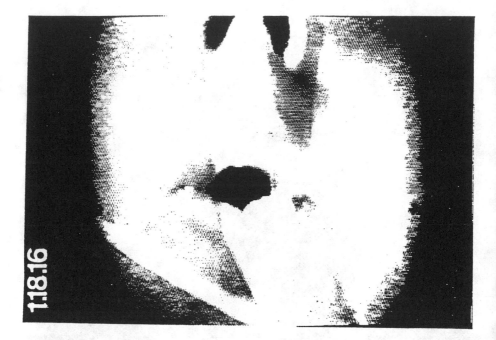

[ɔ] and [ɪ] can-trive [a] [ha] [2]
'trive [a] [ha] [3] 'trive [a] [ha] [2]
[o] and [ɪ] can-trive [a] [ha] [4]
[6]y [7]-----------[5]

The New Music Choral Ensemble (NMCE I) was formed by Kenneth Gaburo at the University of Illinois in 1964. The group quickly became Internationally recognized for its virtuosity and accomplished repertoire of new works. In 1968 Gaburo left Illinois for a position at UCSD. He was joined by four ensemble members. Together they formed NMCE II, patterned after the earlier group. But, a long term involvement with theater and linguistics, and a desire to pursue new regions of musical expression led to the formation of NMCE III in 1969. This group of eight members gave up the music stand for the floor, and the sole focus on the voice for the greater expressive potential of the entire human. It was characterized by such expressions as action-, talk-, gesture-, and theater music. It engaged in such concepts as group composition, heuristics, group dynamics, and the body as a contra-puntal linguistic system.

In 1972, NMCE IV was formed as a resident group within the UCSD Center for Music Experiment under a 3-year grant from the Rockefeller Foundation. Earlier developments directly led to more rigorous research/performance concerns along physiological, acoustical, and structural linguistic lines. There was also active involvement with computer, video, film, electronic, laser, and optical technology. For the first grant year the group consisted of a singer, a mime, a speaker, an actor, a sound-movement-instrumentalist, and an acrobat. As well, the group exhibited a wide range of other talents including set-design, karate, film-making, meditation, and the performance of music from Bach to Indian Ragas.

The second grant year included four performers who devoted themselves to such matters as fine-tuning, multiphonics, video composition, translation, observation, non-interpretive states, focus, awareness, and sound as a means for generating movement. The Minim-Tellig compositions presented in this essay are from this period. The works were written for Philip Larson (M=I #1), Linda Vickerman (M=I #2), and Lin Barron (M=I #3).

The third grant year provided for five dancer/acrobats who embodied elements of all previous groups, added extraordinary new dimensions (e.g., composing with generative grammars), and viewed movement as a means for generating sound.

Within the time span 1964-1976, these groups collectively performed over 100 new works (in some 200 public performances), including so-called 'typical' choral music (e.g., Webern, Schoenberg, Messiaen, Oliveros, Nono, Gaburo, Johnston, Shallenberg, Erickson); music theater (e.g., Kagel); theater (e.g., Beckett, Albee); linguistic compositions (e.g., Thoreen's poems/generative grammars, Brun's Mutatis Mutandis/computer graphics); dance/theater (e.g., Gaburo's My, My, My, ——What A Wonderful Fall), and engaged in on-going research. Some of their efforts may be found on recordings (e.g., CRI, Nonesuch, Ars Nova Ars Antiqua, Lingua Press), and on film and video (e.g., Lingua Press).

——Kenneth Gaburo, Iowa City, 1986

PHOTOGRAPHY BY DAVID MARTIN

**R. Murray Schafer**

R. MURRAY SCHAFER was born in 1933 in Sarnia, Ontario, Canada. He is a composer, writer and educator. He studied at the Toronto Conservatory with Guerrero (piano) and Weinweig (composition). From 1956 to 1961, he worked as a freelance journalist and BBC interviewer in Europe, while editing Ezra Pound's opera *Le Testament de François Villon*. In 1972 he received a grant from the Donner Foundation to research worldwide acoustic ecology. He has also received grants from the Canada Council, Fromm Foundation, a medal from the Canadian Music Council, and a Guggenheim Fellowship.

Schafer's music has its roots in 12-tone serialism, indeterminacy, and mixed-media. He often draws on fields beyond music: the philosophy and literature of many different times and peoples. Schafer has often composed with invented languages or dead languages to emphasize sound over semantic meaning.

Schafer is the founder of the World Soundscape Project involving detailed study of sound environment (noise pollution, acoustic design, aesthetics) and Sonic Research Studio at Simon Fraser University.

In addition, Schafer is the author of important books on music: *Creative Music Education* (Schirmer Books), *Music of the Environment* (Universal Edition), *The Thinking Ear* (Arcana Editions), and *The Tuning of the World* (Knopf). His music is recorded on RCI (Canadian collection) and CRI.

# Language, Music, Noise, Silence

## (A composer's approach to words)

### R. Murray Schafer

When language becomes unintelligible, it enters one of three states: music, noise, or silence. When it is listened to sensuously it becomes music. When meaning is sought and not found it becomes noise. When it isolates completely it enters the zone of silence.

The vast migrations of people today, either by tourism or as refuges, are rendering language increasingly unintelligible. It is shorn of nuance for one whose fluency is restricted to a few hundred words, has become gibberish for the alien and is further "destructed" by technical jargon.

To have become the *lingua franca* of the Western world is not an advertisement for the special efficiency of English but merely the corollary of colonial and imperialistic successes. The widespread use of English today has left it more prone to communication breakdowns than any other language. It is brutalized by commerce, dehumanized by technology, fumbled by non-native speakers and blunted by bureaucratic and academic obliquity. Whole areas of affective expression known to Shakespeare and the translators of the King James Bible have slumped into aphasia.

"People are such poor conversationalists in America", said an English lady to me recently. Of course. You can only push so much vocabulary into a person's head in a lifetime and when half the capacity is given up to professional sublanguage or a native tongue no longer useful, there is less space for the acquisition of material which might enhance general conversation skills.

"I speaking fourteen languages and best from all is English", said the Mittel-European emigrée.

In my country, Canada, native speakers of English make up about one third of the population: twenty-five per cent speak French and twenty-nine percent are emigrants - giving, as may be imagined, a certain haziness to communication. If English is a world language, spoken by increasing numbers of people, it has been reduced to Ogden and Richards' basic 300 words in which clone expressions like "Have a nice day" or "No problem" are forced to carry the burden of a thousand other sentiments. It may not be true ipso facto that greater verbal flexibility leads to more advanced communications, but it is a start. Or is it that we are deliberately protecting ourselves from involvement with others by feigning speech loss?

It is not only while travelling abroad that one flounders in monosyllables: "Me from Canada. Go to Italy. You nurse? Take holiday. Very nice." One can travel the Greyhound bus throughout North America without getting much more satisfaction. On a modern city bus one hears a polyglot of twenty languages in which the only distinguishable and imminently recurring word is "dollar". Of course there are leitmotifs in any culture.

"You are being too severe," said a reader of these pages, "people still communicate." Of course they do: with hands, and shoulders, eyelids and clothes: and above all with music, for this becomes the real social mucilage in an era bereft of words and ignorant of literature – music constantly, to anesthetize the need for articulate contact.

Music. Noise. Silence. The breakdowns of language lead to these states: but they can be positive as well as negative. Who would deny that it is frequently enjoyable to travel in a strange country where not a word of the language is understood? To be alone. To be left alone. To be released from the odious task of having to communicate with others. To hear the vocal surge as pure sound. To become a listener. To hear voices: pleasant voices, angry voices, rasping voices, luscious and succulent voices, asmatic and wheezy voices. To listen to all this mellifluous flowing as if it were a continual singing, accompanied by the orchestration of the soundscape around, beneath and above it.

If it is necessary to communicate (humans being among the most gregarious of animals) it is also frequently pleasant not to. The breakdowns in language assure us of a certain amount of privacy in an era given to increased interference in all aspects of one's life.

In 1965 I went to Simon Fraser University to join a communication department. Communication departments were only invented when communication became a problem. Ironically my first lecture to Communications 100 was a plea for the satisfactions of non-communication. When the information bomb explodes, I asked, where are you going to hide? It is not natural for the human organism to remain one great unblinking eye and ear in the face of overpowerful stimuli. Filters will be sought. Screens will be erected. Invasion will be resisted. And of course this is what has happened in the plethora of alternative and competing information systems (where one would be more logical) as well as the increase in sectarian

106

vocabularies (technocratic, commercial, Black, computerese, etc.) and, as I have said, in the constant tide of new speakers of English, who tend to keep the language in a state of infancy. When everyone in your neighborhood speaks a different language the dialectical pleasures of conversation vanish, leaving only the interior monologue - that is to say, silence.

Language as music, noise, and silence - this is how I have tended to treat it in my works.

In *Patria 1: The Characteristics Man*, which is the first part of an extended series of music theatre pieces I have been engaged in for several years, the protagonist is an emigrant to a new country. Patria (Latin for homeland) is this place, our place, but the emigrant-hero understands neither the language nor the social values of the new land. He tries to make sense out of the things that are said or done to him, often misinterpreting them. This gives the work tragi-comic flavour. Behind him the orchestra plays a frequently ciphered music (for instance there are sometimes secret messages in Morse code rhythms) and a large choir sings a series of extended choruses more or less in the spirit of the choruses of Greek tragedies. The texts of these choruses are taken from classical languages: from the Sanskrit of the *Bhagavad Gita*, from a Babylonian penitential psalm and from Dante's *Inferno*. That these are unintelligible is of no consequence: the tone of inflection gives them their character, sometimes hostile, sometimes sympathetic, for they are sonorous spectators who sit in constant judgement over the hero-victim. Like old wives they never cease commenting on his behavior. By contrast he never speaks a word in the entire work and the only sound he makes is a single sob at the conclusion. It is a story of the seamier side of refugee life -- one that we would like to ignore: but it probably needs telling.

The theme of *Patria: Requiems for the Party Girl*, is also alienation. The protagonist here is a young gay-tragic woman named Ariadne. She is the prototype of those strange harlequinesque creatures one occasionally sees at parties beneath whose gregarious *joie de vivre* one detects obscured signs of terror. Ariadne's desert is her own mind and it can be reached by no telescope, for when we meet her she is a schizophrenic patient in a mental hospital.

Psychiatrists tell us that schizophrenics often speak a language intelligible to themselves and other schizophrenics, though we cannot understand it. Thus in Patria 2 Ariadne and the other inmates speak the *lingua materna* of whatever country in which the work is produced while the psychiatrists and nurses converse along

107

themselves in foreign languages: German, Hungarian, Italian, Norwegian, Spanish, French, Danish, Russian, and Serbo-Croatian - a situation, by the way, which is often true of mental hospital staff. Characters speaking Arabic and Sanskrit also appear in Ariadne's dreams and nightmares and one of these is accompanied by an extended chorus in Tibetan from the *Barbo Thödol*. I should emphasize that what the doctors and nurses say is perfectly logical, though as we are intended to experience the world through the eyes and ears of Ariadne, almost nothing they say makes sense. While the inmates speak English they are by no means always intelligible. Sometimes I have used actual statements of patients heard on personal visits to mental hospitals: "What are you going to do when your mother is a locomotive?" Sometimes I have composed meandering speeches like Markoff chains by using stochastic processes: "I love it in the bathtub with rubber toads crawling out of wrinkled purses ...." As the gossiping voices around her whisper their absurd propositions in her ear, Ariadne, the lone coherent, though doomed, personality in the entire work, comments: "Outstretched hands are rare." Which reminds me of Kafka's comment towards the end of his life when the doctor left his hospital bedside: "So the help goes away again without helping." So much for communication in the modern world.

In other works I have employed language in a quite different manner. The basic text for *Ra*, a later work in the *Patria* series, is in Middle Egyptian. *Ra* is a hierophany lasting from sunset to sunrise in which the audience become initiates and are led through the underworld by priests to witness divine scenes dealing with the sun god's dangerous passage through the caverns of the night. All the gods speak and sing ancient Egyptian. The priests are bilingual, interpreting their utterances to the initiates. My note to the performers explains how language functions here:

> The sounds and images of these texts are different, but that language itself is employed differently here. These are thaumatological or magical texts. When delivered properly they can produce miracles. This is what the Egyptians believed and this is what you must believe.

> In all so-called primitive languages the word encapsulates a strange power and when the correct tone of enunciation is found the power of the word is released to accomplish its desired end. This is very different from the discursive and descriptive forms of language and literature with which you will be more familiar. Modern languages facilitate the presentation of thoughts and the depiction of events. We might call them metonymic, because they constitute an

analogue for reality. Here words *stand for* objects, and the speaker is free to move aside from the objects described to reflect on them or colour them with attitudes like sincerity, credulousness or irony. But the texts of *Ra* are hieroglyphic. They do not argue; they are certainly not logical. They are hard physical presences, palpable and complete in themselves. They do not stand for objects; they are themselves objects, and when uttered properly these objects (gods, spirits) come to life.

Do not shy away from the strange sounds of this language. Deliver its phonetics firmly and with faith that this magic, which is created in the mouth, will be truly effective. When you repeat words or phrases try to hit the right resonance that will release this energy. This is what you must believe when you are performing *Ra*: you are creating and destroying the world with your mouth.

It is a short step from the magic language of Middle Egyptian hieroglyphs to the creation of magic languages of one's own. Already in the prologue to the *Patria* series - a work entitled *The Princess of the Stars* - this had been intimated.

*The Princess of the Stars* is a dawn ritual at a lake in which the principal characters move across the water in large decorated canoes. Musicians and singers are around the shore at various distances from the audience, some as far away as a kilometer. The story, which could be an Indian legend (though it is not) recounts how Wolf comes to look for the Princess of the Stars who is being held captive at the bottom of the lake by an evil character called the Three-Horned Enemy. Wolf invokes the Dawn Birds to help him find the Princess but the Three-Horned Enemy will not release her. At the conclusion the Sun Disc arrives (with the real sunrise) and sets various tasks for Wolf before he can find and be united with the Princess. It is these tasks which Wolf, in various guises, executes in the subsequent series of Patria works, though he will not succeed until the Epilogue - a work yet to be written.

Language contributes strongly to the ritual effect of *The Princess of the Stars*. The gods and animals speak and chant an unknown language or, to be more precise, a series of unknown languages. Wolf chants an invented language incorporating some morphemic and phonetic elements of North-American Indian dialects. This lends it an ancestral dignity but also has a practical significance since Amerindian languages not only have an abundance of long vowels but they contain few labials or other phonemes which do not carry well in the open air. The chorus around the lake chants actual Amerindian words for "star", "lake", "princess", and "wolf". These are not employed syntactically but are colour words, chosen from a cross-section of languages, those of the eastern woodlands predominating.

Another series of colour words is that forming the Sun Disc's welcoming music. Beginning with the ancient Japanese word for sun, *"ohisama"*, sun words follow in a geographical curve around the world through the languages of Asia, Africa, and Europe. The Sun Disc himself chants an invented language with a strong suggestion of Latin cognates.

The Three-Horned Enemy's speech contracts sharply with that of Wolf and the Sun Disc; neologisms, notable for their monosyllabic abruptness of compact vowels and waspish consonants are given additional bite and distortion by means of a loud hailer implanted in the Enemy's costume. A further independent vocabulary is that of the Dawn Bird's chorus, this deriving partly from ornithologists' notebooks and partly from personal listening experience plus imagination.

In *Patria 5: The Crown of Ariadne*, I attempted for the first time a completely synthetic language. The language was originally invented for the novel *Dicamus et Labyrinthos*[1] in which an archeologist, attempting to decipher the ancient language of Ectocretan, becomes trapped in the labyrinth of his own decipherment. At the beginning of the novel nineteen tablets are presented in the strange script of Ectocretan. As the decipherment proceeds, phonetic values are ascribed to the characters and eventually meanings begin to emerge. A few lines in IPA will suffice to suggest the phonetic character:

1.  Oleordi snems
    (Ariadne sleeps)

2.  Ke snems zui snem ui  - o ksuonr
    (she sleeps the sleep of a child)

3.  wuif os ke snems ke rleps
    (but as she sleeps she dreams)

4.  Ke rleps ui  - nuib odr nuisf
    (dreams of love and lust)

5.  of tdusas
    (at Knossos)

6.  ud zui suide kals ui  - tlef
    (on the sunny shores of Crete)

110

As the example shows, the text purports to be about Theseus, Ariadne and the Minotaur. But we can never be sure about the trustworthiness of decipherments which cannot be cross-checked against large amount of additional source material, and since this is lacking the author of the translation meets with scepticism and hostility within the academic profession.

But poetry may be all lies; therefore the curious text revealed by decipherment is taken over as the libretto for *The Crown of Ariadne*. This piece is a dance-drama with music and singers, set in pre-classical times on Crete. It is intended to be presented at sunset on a seashore. Passing into night the work concludes with the burning of the labyrinth and the escape of Theseus and Ariadne by sea. Here I am relying on a certain familiarity with the myth plus the actions of the dancers and actors to render the story clear. Listening to the chanted text would be about as satisfying as listening to an opera sung in the original tongue - no more perhaps, but certainly no less. The actors wear masks and the tone of their chanting, often pinched and whistling, drops at times from head to bowel-tone, to a ferocious growling, below speech, terrifying to hear, reminding us that the Cretan empire, while civilized, was also a brutal autocracy.

Language: music, noise, tone-magic. It is all here whenever the voice forms words. The composer follows the psychographic curve of speech releasing additional energies undreamed of by mere speakers. The Indians spoke of song as a "trail to heaven" in which the footsteps of the singer provided the rhythm while the windings of the path give rise to the turns of the melody. They also believed that a song was a singer's private property, uncounterfeitable and untransmissible. None of this has changed. And beyond the song is silence, the apotheosis of all soundmaking on this earth, and perhaps the supreme joy.

1.     Published by Arcana Editions, Box 425, Station K, Toronto, Canada M4P 2G9

## TABLET ONE

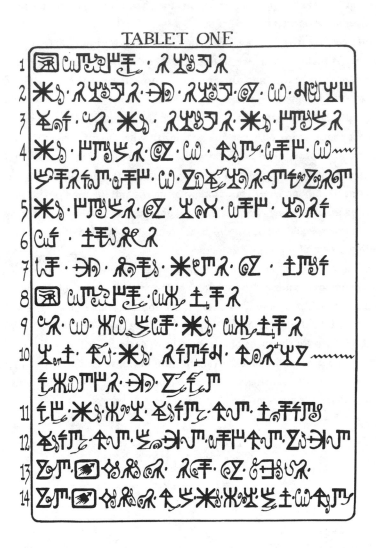

15)
16)
17)
18)
19)
20)
21)
22)
23)

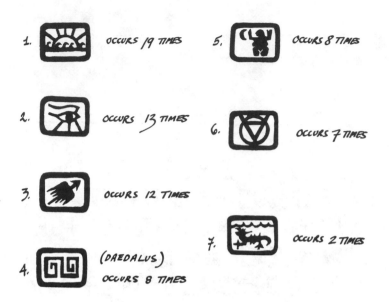

1. OCCURS 19 TIMES

2. OCCURS 13 TIMES

3. OCCURS 12 TIMES

4. (DAEDALUS)
OCCURS 8 TIMES

5. OCCURS 8 TIMES

6. OCCURS 7 TIMES

7. OCCURS 2 TIMES

Each sign is distinctive but there are some conspicuous relationships. Two contain wavy motifs suggesting water. In one a sea serpent lurks beneath the surface; in the other a rising or setting sun appears above the waves. The sun is complemented in another sign by a new moon. This is also one of two signs depicting women, but they are very different. One shows a large-proportioned woman with carefully incised pudendum. The other shows a woman's eye which, while resembling the Egyptian hieroglyph for the verb "to cry" differs in that it faces to the right.

Combining signs 1, 5 & 8, I am reminded of the ancient Aegean and Middle East myth to explain the passage of the sun: each day a hero is born from the sea, rides westward in the sky, is killed, sinks into the sea and is carried eastward by night in the belly of a sea dragon, being vomited up at dawn to repeat the cycle.

114

February 9. I have begun this notebook to record my thoughts as I work on the decipherment. What an achievement if I could do it. Or rather, if I could be the first to do it, since others are also at work on the text. Time will decide everything, cutting success from failure, fame from obscurity. There will be no half measures: someone will succeed, the others will fail. A rival could arrive just ahead of me with the text flawlessly decrypted and my whole striving would have been in vain. We plod in the tunnel, wishing to remain ignorant of rivals. No flash until the end. Supposing the text proves important? Then it explodes like a light show, dazzling men of all races and cultures, changing them.
—And whose name shall we write at the bottom of the program?

---

Feb 12. ALL MEN MAY SPEAK, BUT ONLY THE PRIVILEGED MAY WRITE AND READ WHAT IS WRITTEN — my theme for the Odysseus Society colloquium last Wednesday. — Provoked much discussion. My argument: the art of language is not improved by the expanding habit of literacy but is merely cheapened by it. It is turned into a vehicle for journalism and bureaucracy. Power is stolen from the privileged, from priests and scholars, kings and poets, and is thinly redistributed over a multitude of petty clerks and scribblers. This decline did not begin with the introduction of universal schooling, not even with the invention of the printing press. It began much earlier with the invention of the syllabary & alphabet. For the transition from the intense script of logograms & pictographs to the relative simplicity of syllabic and alphabetic writing was not the accomplishment of scholar priests. One even imagines them resisting its development. It was no deliberate plan of the enlightened then, but happened when illiterate people, with no desire to preserve the sacerdotal character of the written text, came into conflict with literate culture, recognized its power, wanted it for its own uses, and stole it by inventing a simpler form of communication

Today priests and scholars cling vainly to relics from the language museum: arcane and foreign words, dead grammatical forms and involuted expressions, in order to retain some vestige of former prestige. But in ancient times all written words possessed mysterious values. Held above the populace, they were uttered in secret by the initiated. They rumbled with divine and terrible powers. A god or a king was encased in his written symbol and his spirit could be released by those who knew how to breathe it alive. Secret codes and undeciphered languages still hold this power. To decipher them could release terrifying forces from which the common man has no immunity. There are those who believe that altering one tracing of an unknown script could change the world, or even end it.

GRAYSON ARGUED HERE THAT THE EARLIEST WRITING SYSTEMS IN MESOPOTAMIA OCCURED IN THE ECONOMIC NOT IN THE RELIGIOUS SPHERE—

WHAT'S THAT GOT TO DO WITH ANYTHING?!

DREARY DEBATE—

---

ᗜᏟᎳᏘᏋᏔᎌᏘᎯ / ᗜᏟᎳᏘᏋᏔᎳᏘᏘᎯ

There are times when I would like to be able to do this —

We know that there is a certain history of letter reversal in sacred texts, videlicet witches' recitation of the Lord's Prayer backwards. Its purpose is always the same: to reverse the universe and transfer its energy to a new custodian. It functions in accord with the principle of compensation, by which everything that runs its course in nature sooner or later reaches a point where it produces enantiodromia, id est, turns into its opposite. Disordered vocalizing turns by degrees into organized speech as speech runs to gibberish. Nothing has fixed ordering: it moves.

Retrograde motion is a battle with time. It attempts to reverse the line back to the first experience and alter the consequences. Imagine the effects if it could succeed. Thieves would bring presents to strangers; young men would rise out of war graves; books would be magically transformed again into trees.

15/2/78. I remember once seeing a book in which the text was printed as a cipher, the letters of each word being deliberately scrambled by the author. Gradually it became clear that what I had in front of me was one phrase repeated over & over, untangling itself by degrees. Only the first statement was completely unintelligible. In each subsequent repetition the words were righted, first the digraphs or two-letter words, then the trigraphs, and so forth, until in the final repetitions even the longest polysyllables became meaningful.

And I recall my state of mind as I worked through it. Bits of information followed by puzzles triggered my mind into anticipating a thousand possible sequels. Later when the real meaning was known, it was something of a disappointment. No, not a disappointment, for I knew it was correct and true, but somehow a betrayal of the possible, the vague, the hinted at. The loose, freely associative mind of the poet had been made to surrender before the deductive method of the scientist. I knew it had to happen but I was sorry to see it go.

---

18/2. Must a written message mean the same thing at all times to all people? How could it, given personal tastes and public fashions in ideas & values? Pope translates Virgil's "cicadas" as "sheep" in order to connect better with the English reader. The error is deliberate. But how far is one prepared to tolerate such falsification in a translator?

---

Then there are the errors of ignorance, for instance the Pylos tablet (172 B - Kn 02) which describes the function of ⊤ labrys the Minoan two-edged axe. General agreement that the tablet records a ritual slaughter, possibly performed within the precincts of a labyrinth, but disagreement over who is killed and who does the killing.

Furumark (1954): Let labrys fall from the hand of the hero and let the cupbearers bear the blood to the altar of Poseidon.

Meriggi (1955): Let the hero be struck down by labrys and a ceremony of consecration be performed in the Poseideion.

Tou fo meryom, tou fo teh lulsk, tou fo teh lehmet nad te chonc lehls, tou fo syad nad hisgnt, I heva noshiedaf sith tumcose fo sdwor rof oyu, nwustiting titell fo ti ta a mite. Eseth era royu losymbs, royu urte canfisigance, hohtug theiner fo su kwen ti neth. Theiner fo su kwen woh teh sulping larity fo ym elov dowul noe ayd mecobe a rentconai fo rembanremec, a save rof royu dafed mobol, a rackced raj fo urego a bomt, shuped up tou of meryom, tou of teh lulsk, tou of teh lehmet nad teh chonc lehls, tou of syad nad hisgnt, I heva noshiedaf sith tumcose of sdwor rof oyu, nwustiting titell of it at a mite. Eseth era royu losymbs, royu urte canfisigance, hohtug theiner of us kwen it neth. Theiner of us kwen woh teh sulping larity of my elov dowul noe ayd mecobe a rentconai of rembanremec, a save rof royu dafed mobol, a rackced raj of urego, a bomt, shuped up out of meryom, out of the lulsk, out of the lehmet and the chonc lehls, out of syad and hisgnt, I heva noshiedaf sith tumcose of sdwor for you, nwustiting titell of it at a mite. Eseth are royu

losymbs, royu urte canfisigance, hohtug theiner
of us kwen it neth. Theiner of us kwen how
the sulping lariety of my elov dowul one day
mecobe a rentconai of rembanremec, a save
for royu dafed mobol, a rackced jar of
urego, a bomt, shuped up out of meryom, out
of the lulsk, out of the lehmet and the chonc lehls,
out of days and hisgnt, I have noshiedaf this
tumcose of sdwor for you, nwustiting titell of it
at a time. Eseth are your losymbs, your true
canfisigance, hohtug theiner of us knew it then.
Theiner of us knew how the sulping lariety of my
love dowul one day mecobe a rentconai of
rembanremec, a vase for your dafed mobol, a
rackced jar of urego, a tomb, shuped up out of
meryom, out of the skull, out of the lehmet and
the conch shell, out of days and hisgnt, I have
noshiedaf this tumcose of words for you,
nwustiting little of it at a time. These are
your losymbs, your true canfisigance, hohtug
theiner of us knew it then. Theiner of us
knew how the sulping lariety of my love would
one day mecobe a rentconai of rembanremec,
a vase for your faded bloom, a rackced jar
of rouge, a tomb, pushed up out of memory,
out of the skull, out of the helmet and the
conch shell, out of days and nights, I have
noshiedaf this tumcose of words for you,
nwustiting little of it at a time. These
are your losymbs, your true canfisigance,
though theiner of us knew it then. Theiner
of us knew how the sulping lariety of my
lore would one day become a rentconai of

rembanremec, a vase for your faded bloom, a racked jar of rouge, a tomb, pushed up out of memory, out of the skull, out of the helmet and the conch shell, out of days and nights, I have noshiedaf this costume of words for you, nwustiting little of it at a time. These are your symbols, your true canfisigance, though neither of us knew it then. Neither of us knew how the pulsing reality of my love would one day become a rentconai of rembanremec, a vase for your faded bloom, a cracked jar of rouge, a tomb, pushed up out of memory, out of the skull, out of the helmet and the conch shell, out of days and nights, I have fashioned this costume of words for you, untwisting little of it at a time. These are your symbols, your true significance, though neither of us knew it then. Neither of us knew how the pulsing reality of my love would one day become a container of remembrance, a vase for your faded bloom, a cracked jar of rouge, a tomb.

1976.

# SCENE 1

## I WAS IN A CITY I DO NOT REMEMBER.

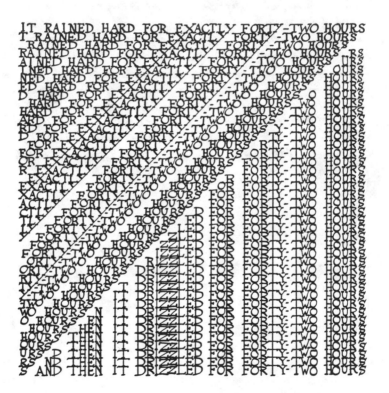

## SCENE 2

I WALKED UNDER THE ENIGMAS OF TALL BUILDINGS

# SCENE 3

OVERHEAD A MAN LEANED
OUT OF A WINDOW AND
CRUSHED CELLOPHANE.
IT SOUNDED LIKE
STARS WASHING
IN WATER.

I WALKED DOWN A QUIET ROAD._____

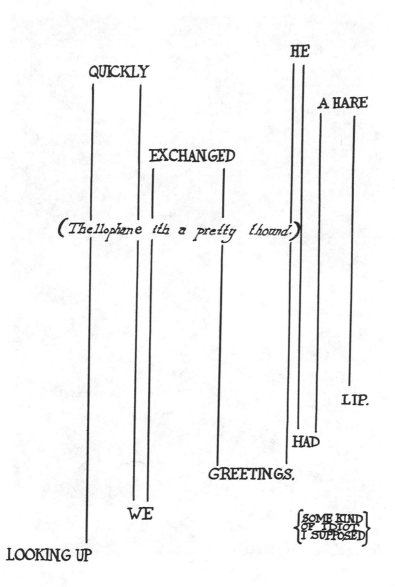

QUICKLY

HE

A HARE

EXCHANGED

(Thellophane ith a pretty thound.)

LIP.

HAD

GREETINGS.

WE

{SOME KIND OF IDIOT I SUPPOSED}

LOOKING UP

125

LEAVING HIM BEHIND, I WALKED ON DOWN THE ROAD PRESSED BETWEEN SHADOWS. HERE AND THERE STREETLAMPS CREATED SMALL POOLS OF LIGHT. I WANTED TO PUSH MY MIND INTO THE DARKNESS, TO FEEL ITS CLAW AT MY THROAT. BUT I WAS AFRAID, AND I REJOICED WHEN EACH NEW LAMP STRUCK THE PATH IN A RATIONAL CIRCLE. THEN I WOULD WHISTLE A LITTLE TUNE. WHEN I STOPPED I THOUGHT I COULD DETECT A FIGURE APPROACHING IN THE DISTANCE...

**Stuart Saunders Smith**

STUART SAUNDERS SMITH was born in 1948 in Portland, Maine. He started studying music at the early age of six. His first professional engagements began at thirteen as a free-lance drummer of jazz, pop, and show bands in his native Maine. These early experiences as a "nightclubbing" musician led him to gradually understand that business criteria are inappropriate standards by which to validate and ennoble art. It is also here that he fell in love with the communal, creative spirit and improvisational techniques of jazz. These two early, formative lessons continue to resonate throughout his career as a composer, scholar, editor and poet, and have led him to create a diverse and unusual body of musical and literary compositions.

Smith eventually left Maine and studied at the Berklee School of Music, the Hartt College of Music and the University of Illinois, where he was awarded Doctor of Musical Arts. He is a past executive editor of *Percussive Notes Research Edition* and is currently executive co-editor of *The Contemporary American Composers Series*.

An overview of Smith's music reveals four, sometimes overlapping areas of concentration: 1) traditionally-notated scores exploring extreme rhythmic complexities; 2) improvisational structures; 3) speech songs; and 4) trans-media systems. (This term refers to a concept or system that is performable by any type of performer, i.e. dancer, musician, actor, etc.)

Smith's awards include the National Endowment for the Arts Composer's Fellowship, the Maryland Artist's Fellowship, the Percussive Arts Society Service Award, the Hartt College Distinguished Alumni Award, and a Pittsburgh Film Forum Grant. His music is published by Sonic Art Editions, and recorded on Spectrum Records, Advance Recordings, and Opus One Records.

Articles on Smith's music have been published in *Perspectives of New Music*, *Interface, Percussive Notes Research Edition*, and *Ex Tempore*. Smith is currently writing *A Composer's Mosaic*, a book of highly personal essays and poems on "the compositional life," and composing *A Vietnam Memorial* for voices, string orchestra, and percussion.

## Percussion in Discussion (Dec. 1984)

## (Language, Percussion, and My Speech Songs)

## Stuart Saunders Smith

*One e and dah*
*Two     and dah*
*Trip o   let*
*Four       dah.*

*One     and*
*Two e and dah*
*Three e    dah*
*Four.*

### I.

Every percussionist recognizes the above excerpt of Western drum language. Western percussionists have developed and are continuing to develop sophisticated and intricate vocal notations to aid in playing beats, visual notations, and exercises. Many of the names of the twenty six rudiments are in themselves vocal notations for the rhythms they represent, like the paradiddle and ratamaque. Rhythmic scat singing among jazz drummers is often the primary method of notation and passing on musical traditions and styles.

As a young drummer, I vividly remember practicing my "Mommy - Daddy" roll and reciting the names of the rudiments as I practiced them. "If you forget how it goes, just say its name to remind you of the rhythm and sticking." This is how Charles Newcomb, my first drum teacher, taught all his young students the basics, - - the rudiments.

When I started to compose I quite naturally built on this concept of words as rhythm. I call the pieces I compose with words "Speech Songs". These songs are for speaking, where the internal rhythms of individual words, phrases, and sentences are the focus.[1] While there may exist, in some of the speech songs, a poetic image, pun, or other linguistic convention, these are incidental to the heart of my concept of a word music using the voice as a drum.

### II.

*Poems I II III* (1970) for five brake drums and narrator is my first text composition. This piece falls in somewhere between the speech song concept and "beat" poetry. The text for this composition originates from my formative years as a composer, and deals with aspects of my earlier life. *Poem I* and *Poem III* evoke images and sounds of the north woods of Maine in winter where I grew up. *Poem II* consists of my thoughts during a break as a night-club musician in a not so crowded bar. In addition, the texts represent a transition from a text with a more or less traditional poetic concept (*Poem I*) to a full-fledged speech song (*Poem III*). *Poem II* is a hybrid of the two.

### III.

*Tunnels* (1982) Version II is a solo music-text-theater composition for any keyboard, string instrument, or multiple percussion set-up.

*Tunnels* is divided into three sections. The first consists of letters, phonemes, and invented words based on the letters in the word tunnels. The second section of the piece is based on the semantic content of the word tunnels. I first looked up tunnels in a dictionary, then I looked up each important word in the definition of tunnels and repeated this process until I built up a huge collection of phrases and words from which to compose the text. The third section is a truncated version of the first section.

### IV.

During the late fall of 1983, I was a homebody. My wife had just given birth to our twins who needed looking after. In the meantime I had just finished two rather big compositions and decided to compose some short pieces. *Some Household Words I-XVI, speech song studes in subtexts: (Exercises in Word ecology)* was the result.

This text composition is a spoken song cycle; each song is based on the sound of a single word or phrase (often the first word in the song). I composed one song a day for sixteen days. The compositional task I set for myself was to investigate the sonic sub-texts often locked up and hidden in a single word. I did this by audibly repeating the word over and over again until it transformed itself into other words and phrases. I composed each song from the list of words and phrases which emerged from the sound of the word I was exploring.

# POEM II for Five Brake Drums and Narrator

### PERFORMANCE NOTES

Percussion: Scrape and grind brake drums with a coat hanger in the right hand and a large bolt in the left. Continue until the cue: "Melt In The Sun," then stop and pick up mallets for the next section.

Narrator: While narrating the first stanza of the poem ("volts and things" ... to "Melt In The Sun") strike a cowbell repeatedly with a soft rubber mallet. Mallet should be held in the left hand while dipping the cowbell in and out of a bucket of water with the right hand. Stop playing during "mica puddles." "Melt In The Sun" should be louder than the rest of the stanza.

Brake Drums

Narrator

rubber
mallets

volts and things vibrating on wires stimulating faded green
neon moons to shine on and off with rainy street mirrors
reflecting on them until the mica puddles Melt In The Sun

♩=c.112

Inside, I'm just sipping my beer,

watching     bar     stools     get     drunk     and

Tempo
Ad. Lib.

Rall.

hearing,  sliding,  cars,  at,  red,  stop,  signs. All which bring up
many questions.

♩=c.112

Molto Rit.

dripping
water

*Bring cowbell out of water while playing the above rhythm. Water should be heard dripping from the cowbell after the last quarter note.

131

X

Porch
Church
Hut
Ch Ridge.

Sell - him - why - him - inch. *

Port of call.
Political.
Poor little cult.

A difficult, whine.

Porch
Church
Hut
Ch Ridge.

Sell - him - - why - him - inch.

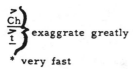 exaggrate greatly

* very fast

This simple procedure often produced startling results. I learned that there are underlying structural connections between sound and meaning built into our language in subtle ways.[2]

*Song X* is a good example of this phenomenon. The theme of this song is the sound "Porch". The two syllables "Por" and "Ch" provide the over-all structuring of the piece. The first part of the piece centers around the "Ch" sound ("t" of the word "hut" and "idg" of the word ridge are related transformations of the "ch" sound.) The second section centers around the "Por" and "Po" sound.

Even though the performance directions state: "Each song should be given its own vocal character which is articulated by the performer's concept of the essence of each text," rhythmically there is less performer disgression than would appear at first glance. The nature of the sounds (words) and there ordering strongly imply certain distinct rhythmic patterns. (It is interesting to note that the other two performers,[3] besides myself, who regularly perform *Some Household Words* treat the internal rhythms very similarly.)

The following is a transcription of the rhythms of my performance of *Song X*.

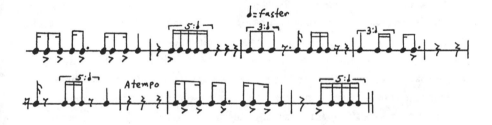

The rhythms of the speech songs are not incidental by-products of an otherwise language based idea. For me the rhythms carry at least equal (if not more) meaning as any linguistic interpretations.

Of course whenever words are used linguistic meanings are not far behind. Many striking images and linguistic connections do emerge from this sound oriented compositional process. A "Porch" is a place where you sit looking out. A "Church" is a place where you sit looking in. A "Porch" is also a "Port of Call" - a social wharf for neighbors to gather and talk. And much of that talk is "Political". And of course things "Political" often degenerate into "Poor little cults" full of people uttering "difficult whines".[4]

I came to feel while composing *Some Household Words* that every word had within it the DNA, if you will, of the entire language from which it is a member. Also, each word has embedded in it its own hidden agenda. A single word is a potential seed from which a multitude of interconnective sounds and images can arise.

## V.

In the beginning there was the word. And in each of our individual beginnings, the first word we speak is our sonic signal of a burgeoning consciousness. Shared reality begins when we learn to name our world.

And our world is words. Language shapes and filters what and how we perceive. Language is our survival tool for constructing a lucid hierarchy out of the second to second sensory anarchy which is our uncensored experience of daily existence. Our shared language is our collective reality - our culture. And each human language sorts out reality in different ways. It is the total sum of all the human languages of the past and present that constitute our species organization of our universe.

As a western composer it is my job, my research, to expand my audiences sense of things. One of the most direct, universal, and radical ways to do this is by enriching and inventing spoken language.

Unfortunately, some people still might think language is a fixed, unchanging object rather than a fluid process of human consciousness interacting with whats out there. This mistaken notion leads to either totally static perceptions or a dull, grey, self-alienation where one has no control over the very thought process itself -- as if the language speaks the person rather than the person speaking the language.

The way we all invent personal endearments and sighs for our loved ones in private, intimate moments, is perhaps an effort to gain more control over our language. In those tender moments only personally invented sounds will do. Using standard words would tend to standardize the uniqueness of the moment. Common words will not do. For our experience is not always common. Sometimes we need language to express and create privacy. (I occasionally wish we would all share our private words, enriching language in one big collective she-bang).

If nothing more, my speech songs are a reminder that language is invented by us and if we are not careful it totally invents us without our awareness or consent. Composing in words helps us regain control, helps us not to be alienated from the center of control: language.

## VI.

*It is the song of speech that I love to sing:*
*The song of everyone,*
*The song of every street,*
*The song of every day.*
*It is the song of speech that I love to sing:*
*The speech song.*

1.  In many of my instrumental works I have tried to capture the seemingly infinite variety of durations, speeds, and articulations of everyday speech. The *Links* series for solo vibraphone comes to mind as an example of this.

2.  I do not mean here to claim that the connections I discovered subjectively are somehow linguistically verifiable. My methodology is artistic not scientific. What I found is in me, that is all I attest to.

3.  Marilyn DeReggi, singer/actress; Timothy Lenk, composer and radio announcer.

4.  I must say that I am very hesitant to make such a linguistic interpretation public. I fear by doing so I may be limiting interpretation rather than encouraging it. The purpose of analysis is not to freeze meaning but to reveal one possible version of a given text or music. My analysis is meant to invite others to invent their own meanings and connections.

# TUNNELS

## Stuart Saunders Smith

**Dedicated to and first performed by
Salvatore Macchia and Robert Black**

PROGRAM NOTES

I once had a dream when I was very little which never left me. In this dream, when people talked, they sounded like musical instruments — this one a tuba — this one a violin — this one a snare drum, and so on. No words came out, just instrumental sounds. I was very disappointed when I woke up to find it was just a dream.

In my speech songs, I reverse the situation. Words come out, but it sounds like music. For me, this music-sense makes perfect sense.

— Stuart Saunders Smith

*Copyright © 1988
By SONIC ART EDITIONS
All Rights Reserved.*

## PERFORMANCE DIRECTIONS

The score is in the form of a text (that is narrated) with six graphic symbols — ( • ; ~~~~ ; O ; [O] ; □ ; [ or ⊔ ⊓ ) that guide the performer in the creation of instrumental accompaniments, unisons, solos, etc. Therefore, this text/score is performed in two ways simultaneously: 1) it is narrated/acted; 2) it functions as directions, along with the six graphic symbols, for a musical accompaniment to the text.

### EXPLANATION OF SYMBOLS

<u>Circles</u> O

Letters, phonemes, or words ((T); (S); (untel)) within a circle are performed only instrumentally. Imitate the actual sound of the circled word or letter as closely as possible with your instrument — imitate its timbre, attack and decay characteristics, pitch, and duration. For example, make a (T) sound as much like a vocal performance of "T" as is instrumentally possible.

<u>Brackets</u> [ ⊔ ⊓

Brackets around letters, phonemes, words, or sentences (⊓T⊓ ; [ET; [Bantam) direct the performer to narrate/act these sounds or words without any instrumental accompaniment.

<u>Periods</u> ⋮

Each period = ca. 2" of music between stanzas, phonemes, letters, etc. (This music is usually a continuation of a word underscored with a zig-zag line.) When a period is enclosed in a bracket, it indicates silence.

[⋮ = ca. 4" of silence

<u>Boxes</u> □

Circled words, phonemes, etc. in boxes ([(ust)]) direct the performer to play and say the word in unison. The music and words of the unisons should be completely fused — i.e., musically imitate every aspect of the word — its timbre, duration, pitch characteristics, etc., as you narrate it.

□ Uncircled letters, phonemes, words in boxes direct the performer to play and say the word in rhythmic unison with instrumental sounds. Each syllable should be accompanied by an instrumental sound. No four consecutive syllables should be accompanied by similar sounds, i.e., no four consecutive syllables should be in the same register, or with the same mode of attack or articulation, etc.

## Grace Notes ♪

All notations with a ♪ indicate a grace note. There are seventeen such notations. ♪ directs the performer to make an instrumental noise. The instrumentalist should use five different noises to be divided approximately evenly among the seventeen indications throughout the composition. Percussionists should interpret the ♪ to indicate a noise or sound not traditionally associated with percussion — radios, found objects of various kinds, etc. There should be five different sources of this kind to be divided approximately evenly among the seventeen indications throughout the composition.

## Zig-Zag Lines ∿∿∿

Words underscored with a zig-zag line ( shun ) are interpreted musically in one of two ways: 1) some aspect of the sound of the underscored word is musically imitated and developed. For example, fins — the performer might improvise/compose an appropriate passage using the duration of the word "fins" with an "s"-like timbre as its basis; 2) the underscored word is interpreted as a performance direction, i.e., the performer improvises/composes an appropriate passage with a word like "declining" or "picking" or "rough" as a description of the music for that passage, i.e., make "declining" music, "picking" music, or "rough" music. The performer should utilize both interpretational modes during a performance. Continue one's performance of a zig-zag underscored word until another musical notation, i.e. a [⋅ or O or ⌐ or ☐ . For example, see page 2 of the score, the word "shuck." The musical interpretation of the word "shuck" continues until [⋅

The performance of zig-zag underscored word continuations need not always consist of continuous sound. The performer can and should add small musical rests to give textured variety and rhythmic interaction with the text.

Zig-zag passages should be contrapuntal in nature.

## TIMING

The visual arrangement of the score communicates formal/conceptual meaning, not implied timings. Letters, phonemes, or words should flow together as if what you are saying makes absolutely conventional linguistic sense. In the score of Tunnels, space does not equal time. There is no implied periodicity or regularity of timing either. The only exception to this general rule is a period ( ⋅ ) equals about 2" of rest or 2" of music. But even here the timings should not be followed slavishly. The total length of the piece should be about 6' - 8'.

## ACTING/NARRATION/VOCALIZATION

Tunnels is a music/text/theater piece. The text should be performed in a dramatic-focused manner. One may perform the opening and closing sections as if one were reciting a profound religious text in Latin. The middle section is performed with a zany gusto.

Tunnels is primarily a musical work. Any overtly theatrical aspects should exist as a result or a byproduct of an intended sound. Avoid overly theatrical interpretations. The text must be heard clearly at all times. The instrumental portion is an accompaniment.

GUIDE TO PRONUNCIATION

All of the non-English text is constructed with letters/phonemes from the word "tunnels." Therefore, pronounce phonemes which are clearly fragments of the word "tunnels" with missing parts like they would sound in the context of the word "tunnels." For example, pronounce "els" as if saying "tunnels" without the "tunn."

Exceptions:

> Pronounce "u" as you.
> Pronounce "ut" as in suit.
> Pronounce "ust" as in boost.
> Pronounce "setun" as seaton.

PREPARATION AND PRACTICE

This composition is not intended as a piece that relies solely on the "spontaneous" aspects of improvisation (although the "spontaneous" aspects of improvisation will undoubtedly be used as one step in the learning/exploring/compositional process).

The first step in learning Tunnels is to thoroughly memorize and develop a vocal interpretation of the text. Then gradually add the instrumental accompaniments, unisons, and imitations of the words, etc. Work carefully and methodically to explore all the performance possibilities inherent in the concept of the piece before choosing your best solution to a given problem. Your vocal interpretation of the text should influence your instrumental solutions to some extent.

Eventually, the performer must be able to coordinate the vocal and instrumental performance of the text so each has an expressive life of its own.

The performer should eventually arrive at a realization of the piece that is repeated verbatim in each performance.

Publisher's Note: After the text and performance directions become familiar, performers may find it useful to prepare a performance score by copying the score pages, cutting away the unessential parts, and affixing them to a sheet of cardstock or posterboard. Permission to copy the score for this purpose is granted by the publisher.

# TUNNELS

Stuart Saunders Smith

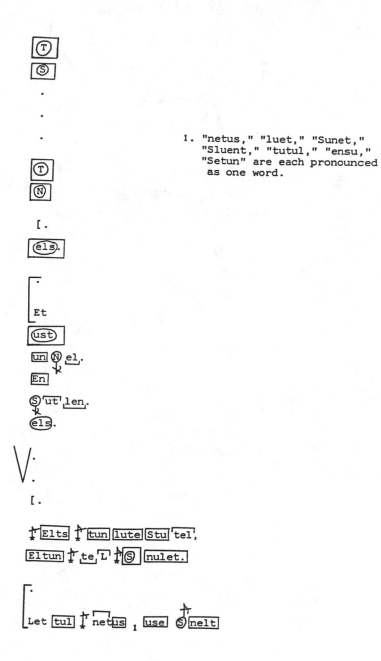

1. "netus," "luet," "Sunet,"
   "Sluent," "tutul," "ensu,"
   "Setun" are each pronounced
   as one word.

⌐luts ↗⌐luet ₁;
En ⌂ ⌐lunes ↗ ⌐sutle⌐⌐sunet₁ Ⓣ.

⌐
  .

  .

⌐Sluent₁ ⌐un Ⓢ↕Ⓣ ⌐nel↗ ⌐tenl ,
⌐lut Ⓢ ⌐lu⌐sten⌐ ⌐Ⓣ⌐tutul₁,
⌐en⌐el ⌐Ⓢ⌐tulu Ⓣ⌐ ₁sul.

⌐
  .

⌐Ten⌐u⌐ ₁tel₁us ?
⌐nust⌐ ⌐ensu₁ ⌐set⌐un₁ ⌐lenus ?
(untel) ?

⌐
    .

    .

  OK.

    .

Tunnels

  .

  .

  .

⌐and a passed⌐ ⌐age .
₁with store₁ shun ,
gave gills weight forth;
only to caps zinc oonjeep,
at eels tongue,
of cast shuck .

  .

  .

  .

Enter orange.

[ .

142

I tick nun
then jaw kelp,
at cussing moons.

molto cresc.

.

.

.

.

.

* Sing, "Blue Moon".
because under the pelvic laces ,
There are, no fins!

.

.

Alone, the inverted Cone
with small openings
ran the instruments
gliding through the antediluvian
declining phase;
because
nest egg pulpits opposed to demand,
Said ready-made theory is USELESS.

.

.

.

That is why Snuffish thought
the WORLD of land
Set apart for the avoidance of intimacy.

.

.

.

.

.
Bantam.

* Actually sing and
play in unison just
the Blue Moon opening
lyric and melody of
the old pop standard
"Blue Moon."

143

(Bantam)

⌐
| ·
|
|_ Paltry.

(Paltry)

⌐·

Potty

·

Are simply idiomatic words,
Under brimless coverings,
which set caps for picking at flaws.

·

·

·

·

·

Ducking metallic salts
not found outside ,
with radiating plates
at red flaps of flesh
hanging live in the water
covered with droll little animals ,
he said,
"The fourteenth letter plus twenty-nine
and one half days equals its
mean density abbreviated M."

Ⓜ

⌐ ·
|
|_ ·

Newark!

·

The Union of South Africa
Veer - oust - schnell - pod - brabble!!

ƒƒƒ

144

[.

*

ƒƒƒ

When will a light touch
the two winged degenerates
infesting the escapement
as pigeons?

.

.

.

.

lide.
lapse.
equivocating.

.

Exist on the rough side of one's
tongue, extending into
the caterwaul.

.

.

Her glide-away organ
Succumbed to
binding shift-elapse;
which change-over Johnny
withheld with his MUTABLE business.

.

.

[of course all above board.

* Continue to play
"brabble" music

** Continue to play
"change-over" music

.

.

.

[Yet.

[.

with impassable trice,
and
spend welcome,
antiqued with whiffet balk
at nark quail stang;
which cock roose of
keep held.


.

[Then

*      {.
       {
       {.

Making assent,
Ashen vast-dad?
[Alas!
[Only mum shallow
blessing suns.


.


.


.

Daystars?

.

[.

Yes, passageways.


.


.

no deeper than a heavy dew.

dim  .

.

.

* Continue to play
"cock" music

[.

[.


146

E lu un nel tus.

[ .

Sulet₁ 'entu'.

[ .

Ten u' tel' us ?

[ .

No

.

Len' ut,

En

El un

Ust ?

Et ?

T

S

T

N

els .

[ .

Ten u' tel, us ?

1. "Sulet" pronounced
   as one word.

147

**Stuart Smith**

SOME HOUSEHOLD WORDS (1984) I- XVI
SPEECH-SONG ETUDES IN SUB-TEXTS:
(EXERCISES IN WORD ECOLOGY)


I

Evening song.
Even
Song even.
Even songings
hear hearing;

.
.

Even more so!

.
.

An ear ring
given
on and on—
(even even,)
(even even,)

.

Long oven
Lovin song.

                              II
mmmmm*        Yesterdays.
                    Gold Ester,

                                    .
                    Summer yes
                    bay bested;

                                    .
                    Hay!
                    Berry mum whirl.

                                    .
                    As Easter
                    loss old yes-sirways
                    with vestments
                    and sand
                    and stirrings
                    and Cape May's
                    and

                                    .                    .


    **        She—her

                                    .
   ***        Air—us

                                    .
                    mmmmmm,

                                    .
      *        Yesterdays.




*Sing opening melody of Beatles' tune "Yesterday" for just the word
Yesterdays.
**Should sound almost like shere
***Should sound almost like eros




                              150

III

*clipped,*    Blanket
*staccato*
.
.

La La lick it.

.
.

Night

.
.

An
Let land tick

.
.

Ocean

.
.

*legato*    Land fill
Blind fold.

.
.

No No No No No

.
.

*staccato*    Blank

.
.

It

.
.

White

VI

*quietly angry*     Hanger

.

.

Close it,
We hurt.

.

Wire celery,
Cardboard anger.

.

Shirt
Wall hangings.

.

Closet chop suey.

.

.

Suicide.

152

VII

Windows
in doors
ill.

.

Lettus lace
as mocha din
in how
beans winnow.

.

.

Frost flowers.

.

Smoking or ice or
out of low king mores.

.

Lattice

.

.

Window, <u>my</u> sill.

## XII

*lyrical* I
E
ket
N T̂ ger.

Hâ win ish,
P̂ lan
at Co
T̂ or.

Ven dows fin I Ays ing o,
Fu t̂er ŝs ear e ong.
Mo dif t̂ foo,
Mo dif t̂ foo,
L ors cull o di,
Do so val
An go re lose
Ga lee a p̂ers,
Ga lee a p̂ers,
Gen T̂ als,
Ce,

I.

*The accented letters and phonemes should have a sharp, percussive quality.*

XIV

* When we go,
  Plants live
  on green heron wind.

  When we call,
  hungry errands,
  one week old, answer.

  When winter hung be Air
  me and slide homer in,
  Then redhot liver and sleeping there we cold.

                                    *lyrical*

*lyrical until the last line, which should be spoken as if saying
"redhot momma" in a bluesy, rough voice with some guttural fry.*

155

## XVI

\* I sigh'n sigh
in between
sea lence 'n open spaces.

.

.

I E len in Sigh Sounds,

.

As slence stuffing sky
with sea sigh since and then,
thinks its own limits,

.

on an Island of

.

E—Sea—L—lence
I—sigh—L—lence

.

.

And side.

*with a very lyrical voice*

156

**Spaces**

Michael Brewster

MICHAEL BREWSTER was born in 1946 in Eugene Oregon. He was educated in Saõ Paulo Graded School in Saõ Paulo, Brazil. In addition, he studied at Pomona College and The Claremont Graduate School, both in Claremont, California. His works have been exhibited in museums and galleries throughout the United States and Europe. He has had one person shows at such institutions as The Walter Phillips Gallery (Banff, Canada), The University of Massachusetts (Amherst, Massachusetts), The Tyler School of Art (Philadelphia, Pennsylvania), The Minneapolis College of Art and Design (Minneapolis, Minnesota), The Galleria Del Cavallino (Venice, italy), The Modern Art Gallery (Vienna, Austria), Corps de Garde (Groningen, Holland), The La Jolla Museum of Contemporary Art (La Jolla, California), The Museum of Contemporary Art (Los Angeles, California), among others. In addition, his works have been presented in such important group exhibitions as the Whitney Museum Biennial (New York, New York), and in numerous group shows at such institutions as Artist's Space (New York, New York) and The Los Angeles County Museum of Art (Los Angeles, California).

Michael Brewster has created an exciting and original series of works which he has called "Acoustic Sculptures." He has described each of these works as constituting "a field of palpable sound volumes, of differing sizes, densities and rates of excitement." In works such as *Configuration 010*, *Standing Wave* and *Synchromesh*, the viewer actually moves through the artwork rather than around it, as in a more traditional sculptural situation. In addition, he has created works which require viewer participation. In *Press on for Sculpture* and *Touch and Go*, the listener/viewer himself must activate the sound structure in order to experience it.

Michael Brewster has taught at Bradley University in Peoria, Illinois, Pomona College in Claremont California and LaVerne College in LaVerne, California. He is currently an Associate Professor in The Claremont Graduate School in Claremont California. He maintains a sound studio for his research in Venice, California.

# Gone To Touch

## Michael Brewster

Looking back: the evidence had been there all along, all over the place. The telltales had gone undetected, overlooked. I hadn't recognized them as parts of the picture. The plot had been so unexpected. I hadn't been ready for it. Most of those minor incidents had been clues. Once I got wise, I could spot it over and over again, all over the place, the same "M.O." applied to every stage of my game. By then it was too late. Its effects were in full control. Even my own mode of operation had felt its muscle. Pulled off by a single undercover operator, it had been an inside job. My whole outfit had been framed systematically, top to bottom, right under my nose. Laying low until the end, the culprit had not shown its hand until the last minute. Coming out on top, unexpectedly, that secret agent had been a classic Sleeper.

My operation had been infiltrated early on. Just when it began is hard to say. That peculiar hijacker had been a stowaway, possibly on board right from the start. This expose begins in early November of '84, on a less than ordinary day. Instead of the crisp shadows and brilliant blue skies that we've come to expect of our So.Cal. winters (usually our best season) that day the light was white and flat. Under a lid of unbroken clouds, nothing stood out. It looked cold, but it wasn't. It was a day, like so many others, when things were not as they seemed.

Late that Wednesday afternoon, I wrapped up my duties in the outback to the East of Los Angeles, and rolled down the hill to the freeway in my derelict Honda. Two hundred thousand miles and nine years in beach parking lots had left its little body bent and rusted. It looked like a wreck, but it wasn't. I had lost all interest in its body years before, but I still took good care of its insides, which I had upgraded at every overhaul. It looked like it couldn't get out of the garage, but it was "*hot*" under the hood. Its battered body camouflaged an oversize engine, a superior transmission, and a few other improvements that made it extra agile and quick. That little wagon was a true Sleeper. Its appearance denied its performance. It looked like hell, but it went like hell. People just wouldn't believe what they saw it do. Sleepers are surprising.

Turning at the signal, windows closed up against the noise, I rolled into the on-ramp. Popping the clutch, we roared up the slot at one-third throttle, leaving the end "at speed," with power to spare, alongside a rolling wall of trucks. A Sleeper car is handy on the freeways. It helps you fake out those big truckers, who like to cut us little guys off on approach, closing us out of the openings. With a car like that you can catch them off guard and slip right through. Bobbing and weaving I sparred my way through their ranks. Then, drifting easily across the next three lanes of cars, I settled down in the fast lane of the "San Berdoo" freeway. We were inbound, rolling West on Interstate-10, headed across town to the far edge of Los Angeles, fifty-four miles away. Running home, with only one stop to make before holing-up in my headquarters at the beach.

I was going to see a man about a job. I put in my ear plugs: This was going to be a Real Job. I needed to keep my ears clean. Not a spin-off Straight Job like the teaching position I had just left, nor an Odd Job as an inventor-handyman to make up for low money, but a Real Job, doing what I really do, making Sculpture "out of" sound effects. The painter, Dan Douke, whose own straight job included directing the Art Gallery at the California State University at Los Angeles, had invited me to listen to his two rooms to see what I might make of them. That was why I had to pamper my ears: to have them ready to "take a good listen."

The ear plugs would protect my hearing from the road noise, helping to keep my ears open and sharp. All that heavy noise would blunt their abilities, closing the threshold up, defending them from the roar of the engine and the pounding road. I needed to keep them as open and sensitive as possible to check out my new subjects. I didn't know what to expect. I was going to listen to those rooms to see what acoustic material I might discover within their layout. I'd be hunting for their echoes, and any other sonic incidents they might conceal. With a little luck, it would become another case for an Acoustic Sculpture.

I was still fond of the old car, loud and beat-up though it was. We'd put in a lot of time together. We'd gone the distance together. Yet it could still perform surprising maneuvers, particularly because nobody suspected that it could. It's body was a complete disguise. Like I said, its appearance denied its performance. It was the perfect Sleeper: the best of its class, but you couldn't tell by looking. It looked weak, but it sounded strong. There is more to a Sleeper than meets the eye.

I'd been fascinated by the idea of Sleepers, off and on, before, and became so again after I discovered that one had wormed its way through my project. Sleeper is the name for something excellent that has been unrecognized, unexpected, or unnoticed, which eventually comes to light, finally getting or giving its due. There are all kinds of them around us: the unnoticed play, the unknown champion, the unseen spy, the "late-bloomer"; all are unexpected winners, including my own secret agent.

Sleepers don't look like winners. Their talents are disguised. They tend to look ordinary. They don't attract attention. When they dress-up it's in plain-wrap. You can't know what to expect. Play it by ear. You have to watch out for them. Laying low until the last minute, they'll sneak up from behind to win, without fanfare. You have to pay special attention. Keep your mind open. It takes some imagination. Sleepers are hard to spot.

You can't know a Sleeper ahead of time. Only a thing whose excellence has been unknown can qualify. It has to earn its peculiar title. Sleepers are named after the fact, looking back. They fit many descriptions, and exist in many different places. But they always occur in the same way. Even if they don't look alike, they all act the same. They all follow the same course on their way to the top. Slow starters, they "come-on" gradually, taking a long low route, "peaking-out" real high, all of a sudden. Shy, but mercurial, that's how they do things. It is their "M.O.", the pattern of their behavior.

Such a pattern is called an *envelope*. It is a graph of how something begins, continues, and ends. It charts a trajectory through time, picturing the rate and level of its rise and fall in terms of attack, decay, sustain, and release. An envelope traces a profile in time that describes the *shape* of an occurrence.

You can spot a Sleeper by the shape of its envelope. It's a matter of timing. The shape of its "attack" is the kicker. Sleepers don't attack. They're too slow. They approach. The shape of their rise time is long and low, culminating suddenly in a mercurial peak. When it comes to uncovering a Sleeper it's what's up front that counts. The aftermath has no bearing on the matter. Some Sleepers hang around, others split.

As an idea, the shape of their behavior can take it from a lot of angles. It's very flexible. It can serve as the format for a strategy or an ethic; it can be a refuge or a pitfall. As an adolescent, I had looked to it as a model, finding virtue in its modest persistence, and style in its restrained vigor. Earlier, at puberty, I had taken solace in its assurance of an unpredicted but eventual climax. Much later, after I'd discovered its imprint all over my sculpture, I felt that its profile looked more like a picture of the "snake in the grass."

My acoustic sculpture, *Touch and Go*, had been hijacked in the making. Its course and consequences had been rerouted. Not by some agent acting like a Sleeper, but by the Sleeper's envelope itself. The Sleeper had thrown its shape all over my piece. Unbelievably, I'd been done in by a *pattern*. I'd become surrounded by the Sleeper's M.O.

An envelope can be the cause of an event as well as the effect of one. Either way, it is the shape of the surrounding circumstance, which the envelope can record or specify. When an envelope directs the shape of an occurrence it functions as a modulator, controlling the variations of the event. A modulator *envelope* causes things within its reach to vary in its own image, muscling them into its own pattern.

Envelopes and modulators, that's what I'd been thinking about that first day, cruising along on the freeway, where we Angelenos do much of our thinking. I had been studying about how to use them to fabricate and control sounds long before I knew anything about this Sleeper's scam. That day, I had been reflecting on how the repeated superposition of the same envelope, over and over again, would configure situations that could actually "grow their own" change and variation. You can get into some mighty "far" places hurtling along up there in those freeway gasses. I was "brought down" in the nick of time, forty minutes to the West, by bright brake lights dead ahead.

There's always a "slow-down" in front of Cal State L. A. It's built into the freeway. The road swerves left and downhill at the same time, then bends back to the right and uphill. Just before the traffic thickened, I veered off to the right and made my escape, shifting down through the exit ramp to ground level. Pausing to repace my attention, I rolled down the windows and took in some air, readjusting to the surface rate. Turning at the signal, in low gear, I began the coiling approach around the college buildings searching for the visitor's place to park. It was well hidden, but I found it. Getting out of the car, I pulled out the ear plugs and submerged into the flood of local noise. Now on foot, I started out through unfamiliar territory, reckoning my uncertain approach to the art building. I didn't know what I was looking for. I didn't have a description. When I got there I understood why. The building was government issue: faceless and indescribable.

Once inside, I spied the gallery entrance before I spotted the stairwell, and decided to eavesdrop on my subjects before going upstairs to meet Dan in his office. I wanted to grab a sample of the room's voices. Even a quick "take" would give me some idea of the range and power of its resonances. Like a throat, a room will overlay its own resonances on the sounds inside it, modulating them with its own "voice."

166

Strolling into the gallery through its glass doors, I crossed a tight vestibule and slipped behind a baffle that screened a narrow floor-to-ceiling slot, the corner "doorway" of the front gallery; a squarish room, 18x20, painted battleship grey and hung with very large landscape paintings. Diagonally across from the entrance, where the rear wall stopped short of the corner, was another floor-to-ceiling gap that opened to the back gallery; a rectangular room, 18x24, also painted grey and hung with large thickly painted landscapes. It was a little deeper than the front space but in plan view it looked like its mirror image. Like the front room it was open at two diagonal corners, where the walls had been stopped short. The door slot in its rear right corner opened onto a most improbable and peculiar gallery space. Only five and a half feet wide, with glass doors making up its outer wall, this space flanked both the principal rooms. It ran fifty-four feet straight to the front, bending to the right to meet the vestibule. It seemed a strange and unreasonable item.

The floor throughout the gallery was off-white linoleum tile over concrete, and its eleven foot ceiling had been softened with acoustic tiles glued directly to the cement overhead. Neither of the rooms held any space captive, ducted as they were to each adjoining space through the access slots. The two main rooms were buffered and linked on their outer and front sides by that glass-sided corridor and the vestibule. Their air was cluttered by a low "whoosh" noise broadcasting from the air vents along the top of the left wall. I doubted that I'd be able to hear much of the room's voicings above it. It would certainly mask off all the quieter responses.

Furtively, I clapped my hands a couple of times, and listened for the echoes. I also let loose a couple of whistles, which brought forth the gallery sitter, glaring. Turning my back, I stonewalled her. I needed to hear these rooms' voices. This was my research. These resonances would be my allies, my informants. In fact, some would be the actual physical building blocks of my sculpture. Each room resounded differently, but both responded with padded, composite replies. The echoes were there, but they were lower in frequency than I'd expected, shorter and weaker than I'd hoped for. They returned after curious little pauses, as if reluctantly let go. There was something peculiar about their behavior. I couldn't see it, but I could hear it. There was something mysterious in their voices.

The sitter was watching the back of my head. I could feel her gaze. Feeling like I'd stumbled into the wrong neighborhood, I ducked-out through the back opening, shaking my head in disbelief at that long, skinny, peculiar room. Its glass wall made it seem wider than it was. It was a very fast place. Like an exit tunnel, that hallway gallery propelled me forward, turning me loose in the vestibule. It left me a little off balance. I tumbled out the entrance and headed up the stairs.

That corridor was the tattle-tale. It gave it all away. It was a too familiar story. This room, "retrofit" like so many other college art galleries, had started out as a class-room. Conscripted out of studio duty long ago, stripped and white-washed, it had been outfitted with regulation track lights and sitter's desk, and pressed into display-duty, at the front. It was well preserved, but it looked a little worn. I sensed that it had served under several regimes. Its surfaces had seen a lot of action since its early days in art production. The often hasty reforms of each occupation had been pancaked over with loads of drywall compound and latex paint. Apart from a few telltale tucks here and there, those piecemeal face-lifts could no longer be seen on its surfaces. But I didn't have to be a detective to hear the irregular scars on its voices. Nothing specific, but enough to know that this room was a veteran. There had been more than one cover-up.

Upstairs Dan and I talked for about an hour, discussing the logistics of this job, joking about the funny aspects of some previous pieces. Dan was very easy to work with, truly a gentleman. We talked schedule, fee, publicity, costs, payments, all those awkward issues, with ease and understanding. I thought it was pretty refreshing. Dan thought it was normal.

He was concerned that the rooms would be adequate, if not interesting to me. I said I'd "cased" them on the way in, troubling his gallery sitter with my "noise tests." I was concerned about their slow responses. They weren't "giving good echo." I suspected that those big paintings blanketing the walls were soaking up the reverberations that I would need to make this work. I needed to make noise in there again, louder noise, before the day was out. But I'd really have to hear it when it was naked, to be sure.

Acknowledging my penchant for burying sounders in the walls, Dan repeated his assurance that I could make all the wall chops and cuts that I might dream up. I replied that I now preferred to *inflect* the change on the rooms, using the lightest touch possible. I wanted to keep all my modifications superficial, if not actually airborne. I'd like to avoid making more than one hole in the walls. I would, however, have to rearrange the gallery's electrical system, which I would put back together afterwards, guaranteed.

Later, under Dan's official shield, I made some louder test noises, walking throughout the gallery shouting and clapping, getting more echo with the stronger signals. Dan introduced Paula van der Lans, the sitter. She wanted to know just what was going on. I explained that we were thinking about putting in a sound installation, continuing the series I called the Acoustic Sculptures, begun in '71; all of which have been based on the spatial effects of *standing waves*. This wave-form phenomena, so named by physics, can expose the dimensional properties of sound, showing the size of its wavelengths, by making sound waves seem to stand still in space, holding their place in fields of distinct and varied concentrations.

I had been clapping my hands, whistling, and hooting, because I was trying to learn a little about how these rooms performed acoustically. You could say I was auditioning the rooms. I wanted to see how they acted around certain sounds. I needed to hear what kind of echo these places could deliver because a standing wave depends on the effects of a sustained echo or reverberation to show us its stuff.

The usually fugitive nature of sound can be arrested, I explained, by bouncing the wave fronts back upon themselves. It's a bit like trapping the sound within its own reflected image, its echo. Its a matter of alignment. The opposite-moving wave fronts must intersect each other in phase, every step of the way. Always in flux, the potential of any point in a sound wave is never static, consistently becoming either more positive or more negative. A wave form "stands" when the correspondence of opposing fronts is congruent, perfectly matched, with every positive going portion neutralized by its opposite "equal," the negative-going portion, causing the sound to seem to hang in place, stilled as if strobed.

I set up these fields of standing sound so that we might wander around through their audial geography, discovering within the effects of acoustic sound another class of sculptural experience: spatial sensations of dynamic, non-solid volumes. The sculpture I offer is a set of percepts we get from the spatial effects of sound when it is modulated by a surrounding enclosure. I explained to the sitter that you could say that these sound fields placed each viewer in the position of "the figure in the landscape." A landscape that can only be "seen" from the inside, by walking your ears through each part of its terrain. That explanation seemed to do away with her skepticism. Throughout the exhibition, she acted as a most helpful guide to this new territory. Her work with the public was invaluable. I owe both her and Dan Douke much gratitude for the whole thing.

These rooms are a tough pair, I said to Dan. Their mysteries might be hard to crack. This was no open and shut case. I'd have to come back to listen-in when the rooms were vacant and bare, between shows. He hoped it wouldn't be too tough, suggesting that perhaps I could use something already on my shelf, to keep it simple, especially in light of the budget. I'd give it a shot, I said, even though the rooms sounded pretty weary and slow. I could probably figure something out to boost those tired acoustics. I welcomed the work. I'd been feeling neglected, and needed the exercise. Unwittingly, I said I had a hunch these spaces might be Sleepers. We left the place laughing, going out through its glassed exit hall, unaware of the upcoming irony.

After a quick inquiry at the printers nearby, I steered the little Honda through the gauntlet heart of Los Angeles and rolled on home to my hideout in Venice, loony-land by the sea. It would be good to be back in the saddle again, no matter how modest the deal. I was pleased, but I wasn't excited. I didn't want to just "plug-in" an old piece, but I couldn't afford to lose my shirt again, either. At the end of that first day things didn't look very promising.

Looking back, however, that project and its hijacker really opened things up for me, even though I did lose my shirt, again. That winter must have been the Season for Sleepers. From that day on, they popped up, in one form or another, all over the place. Many were old ideas, long in the works, which resurfaced and bunched together, now making a different kind of sense than before. Following their lead, I launched into rich territory.

That first day marks the beginning of the Sleeper's infiltration, the coup that turned out to be my liberation. I'd like to declare it a holiday. But a Day of the Sleeper would never be a very important holiday. It's profile would be so low that even the banks would stay open. You wouldn't be expected to visit, eat or spend too much. So low key, it would probably look like any ordinary day. People would forget about it. It might get good after dark, but who knows? Sleepers are unpredictable. They do get pretty hot once they're on their final approach, but with Sleepers it's hard to say ahead of time.

During the following weeks I pondered the case, hitting it from all angles. It was tough. All I had to go on was a sketch of its footprint and the few things I'd overheard. Going back to the drawing board, time and again, I drew scaled diagrams and perspective views of the rooms from off-beat points of view, trying to decipher the directives of its floorplan. Eventually I recognized the obvious, seeing a simple solution that would incorporate all the parts of that floorplan, without contradicting the architecture's directions to the viewers.

170

My plan reversed the usual traffic pattern by starting at the front end of the "exit gallery". The installation would be set up to provide two sequential, timed experiences, each winding-up in one of the main rooms. The two situations would be identical in format: start, approach, enter, inhabit, depart. The hallway space would be the approach to the back chamber, which would, in turn, double as the approach to the front chamber. Each approach would begin with a touch-sensitive switch that would trigger a sound field on down the line, culminating in the room at its end. With signal lighting, switching and signage to direct us, the sounding sequences would draw us through the rooms. All these *accessories* would be interconnected through an exposed electrical conduit. Their functions would be coordinated by a bunch of clock circuits on a central timer board, hidden, with the sound and envelope generators, inside the hollow end of the extra thick middle wall.

Carrying my tone generators out to the galleries on countless nights, I set up standing waves of different sizes and character. I teased and tested their acoustics, trying to get a grip on the peculiar and varied reactions they voiced. I probed the reverberations by walking and re-walking through the volumes. I listened for the strongest resonances, retracing my steps. Like I said, their resonances were my material, but it took a lot of legwork to decipher them. In those standing fields the only way to know what is "over there" is to go over there and walk through "over there." You can't hear "over there" from over here. I found that even though the two rooms looked alike they didn't sound the same. Not mirror-images, they were actually the "flip-side" of each other. Acoustically they behaved in very opposite ways. What one could reflect the other could only absorb. What one could repeat, the other couldn't even recall.

Eventually my questioning did turn up the answers. The clues had been in its voices all along. The legwork paid off. Now I knew what each room could do. I had learned their habits. I could see through the layout. As echo chambers, the galleries had similar features but different M.O.s. Now I had their numbers, but I was missing the twist that would tie them together at the scene. Nothing made sense until I went at it backwards, walking the floor plan in reverse, against the flow of traffic. Coming in from behind, their circumstances seemed to fit together. From that angle I could see the whole scheme. *Touch and Go* put the two chambers to work in tandem. Each housed a different sound field. Our passage through its interiors consisted of a 3 minute arrival and a 2 minute departure. A full circuit took under 6 minutes.

171

The installation reversed the gallery's usual patterns, altering our course right from the start. Just inside the glass doors our path was deflected by a little paper sign pointing: THIS WAY-->, turning us to our right, into the front leg of the glassed corridor, directing us to enter through the gallery's usual exit. We were facing a standard electrical switch box mounted, belly-high, on the wall across from us, highlighted by a red spotlight. On its faceplate we could read the word "TOUCH" in flickering red light. This was the beginning of the piece. Touching the switch plate set off the first sequence. The red invitation on the faceplate was replaced by the green command: "GO 3 minutes," and, as the red spot faded down, the first sound field came up in the back room. The wavering sound came pulsing towards us, as if beckoning, from the far end of the corridor, which now glowed with red light.

Turning at the signal, we started our approach into the hallway. Just a few feet ahead, its width was two-thirds blocked, on alternate sides, by three pipe railings, hip-high, spaced about three feet apart. These were the Training Bars. The path they contoured was a suggestion of how to proceed: walk slowly from side to side. They formed the actual threshold of the piece. Placed where the sound field first became evident, their crooked passage introduced us to the simplest of the upcoming sensations. By bending our path in a U-turn across the hallway, the Training Bars slowed us down enough to readjust our perception and guided our heads through a place where the pulsed sound seemed to concentrate and float momentarily, like a bubble of thicker air. It was just a hint of things to come.

Taking the cue from the Training Bars, our path continued to trace a slow "S" down the corridor, carrying us side to side through more pronounced zones of pulsing sound that we found hovering along the sides of the passage. The field seemed to thicken substantially near the end of the hall. Once there, most of us, abandoning our training, picked up speed and veered left, entering the back room from behind, through the rear door-slot.

The place looked empty, but it sounded full. It was loaded with a much louder, more distinct field of sound, thickly alternated with pulsing volumes. We faced a small black loudspeaker directly across from our entrance, mounted in the back corner, belly-high. The sound source was lit by a red spot, while the opposite side of the room was lit by a pink flood which cast a curved perimeter on the walls and floor. The lighting was low, on the dark side, but navigable. Mostly red wavelengths, it made the air look a bit granulated.

The sound was coming out of the tiny speaker at about 100 decibels, c scale. Pulsing at 4 beats per second, it was the mix of two tones, 205 herz and 209 herz, between G and A in the third octave, cycling on for 10 seconds, and off for 1.5 seconds, continuing for three minutes after we touched the switch. The sound field was the product of two wavelengths, of almost equal size, a 5 foot 4.5 inch wave modulated by a 5 foot 3 inch wave.

The 10 second pulse was enveloped into a quick 0.5 second attack, a high smooth 6.5 second sustain, and a slow, steadily falling 3 second release. The sound's envelope was not the shape of a Sleeper. Its front end came up fast and steady right from the start. Its shape was more like the pattern of a Keeper, holding its profile long enough to allow us to scrutinize it. In here you listened to the fullness of the pulse. The back room had an intimate touch. In here you could feel the sound. Its three minute field brought the space in, close around us, providing sensations of the "near-field," of "here," our immediate surround. With each stop we would arrive at another aspect of the pulsed field. It helped to stop and start, bobbing and weaving our ears slowly through its varied terrain. In here you moved quickly during the interval, but slowly during the pulse.

The back room had a varied and regional response, reinforcing different aspects of the signal at different parts of its geography. Over the years its walls had become padded sandwiches of various materials, each with its own peculiar composite resonance. Now some portions of the walls worked against the others, cancelling their resonances. There were occasional voids, dead hollows, in the sound field. One, curiously, was only about a foot in front of the speakers. It was adjacent to one of the loudest portions of the field. The reverberations mixed, unmixed, and remixed, unpredictably, throughout the cavity. In some places the pulse beat appeared to change its rate, while other spots were populated by ringing harmonics.

The absence of the field during the 1.5 second intervals underscored the emptiness of the room. The pulses trailed little, if any, echo. Although it appeared quite full and resonant in the presence of the signal, the back room couldn't keep an echo up on its own. Built piecemeal, it had been dampened, if not rubberized, by its "checkered" past. The back room responded reluctantly, acknowledging only the longer wavelengths. Its range was confined to those frequencies with which most of its surfaces vibrated sympathetically. This room now worked by soaking; absorbing the invading sounds instead of bouncing them away. The only reason it could support a field of standing waves was that the speaker was pumping its volume with more energy than it could absorb.

Cut-off at three minutes, the field disappeared as the lights dimmed down. A red spot faded up on a second touch-switch, mounted belly-high on the outer wall of the back room, a few feet forward of the rear door slot. Like the first, its faceplate said "TOUCH" in flickering red light. This switch triggered the sculpture's second and final sequence. The sign changed to the green command: "GO 2 minutes," causing the red spot to fade down, while bringing up the sound field in the front room. We could hear its short strident bursts, calling repeatedly from around the corner. Turning at the signal, we made a fast approach to the door slot, entering the front room, again from behind.

The place looked empty, and it sounded empty. It staged a field of departing echoes. This room was laid out like the first. Directly across from our entrance, another small black loudspeaker was mounted in the front corner, belly-high. It was lit by a red spot, while the opposite side of the room, the reflector, was lit by a pink flood.

The sound was coming out of the tiny speaker at about 110 decibels, c scale. It was the mix of two tones, 350 herz and 250 herz, F fourth and B third, cycling on for 0.6 seconds, and off for 2 seconds, continuing for two minutes from the moment we touched the second switch. The sound field was the product of two wavelengths, a 3 foot 1.5 inch wave modulated by a 4 foot 5.0 inch wave.

The envelope of its 0.6 second bursts was all attack, cutting-off abruptly at the peak in a sudden release. Although it was all "front-end," its contour was also not the shape of a Sleeper. Coming up so fast and strong from the start, this envelope looked like a Comer, but it turned out to be a "Flash in the Pan." As soon as it hit its peak it collapsed and was gone, making room for the field, which took place during the interval. It was made by the after-effects of each burst. The signal lasted just long enough to charge the front room to its full resonant capacity. Its sudden release cut loose a field of fading echoes that was renewed once every two seconds, just before it faded away, by another burst of sound.

The front room seemed tighter and more vibrant. Its walls must've been tauter, enabling it to support a long-lasting echo. In there you listened to the hollow, in the interval. The fade somehow introduced the percept of distance. The longer-lingering echoes contoured more remote borders. The front room brought you glimpses of a "far-field" experience, of "there," the remote surround. In the echo

174

field, the spatial properties were evenly dispersed. It helped to stop and start, slowly sweeping our ears around its contours. In the front room we moved during the pulse, pausing in the interval to listen to the departure of the local echo.

The two minutes went by pretty fast. The sound ran out just as we were catching on, trailing one lasting echo as the lights dimmed down. We walked out through the entrance into the now greenish light of the vestibule. To our left, signalled by the red spot, the first touch-switch was reset, ready for another tour. We could give up, and get out. Or, we could go around again. I've always favored the repeat. Once is never enough; it's just a glance. Do a double take. Read this story over again, from the beginning.

The Fine Arts Gallery was hidden inside Cal State L.A., it did not attract attention. Though only fifteen minutes east of downtown Los Angeles, it was out of the way. Open to the public during the limited hours of noon to five, Monday through Friday, it did not make itself available. Yet, ironically, *Touch and Go* itself was not a Sleeper. It was noticed right away, and was favorably reviewed. It was not neglected, but it wasn't celebrated. It didn't get any more attention at the end than it did in the beginning. There was no glorious peak. It's not easy to be a Sleeper.

The "Real Job," as it turned out, was the squeeze the Sleeper's pattern put on me. Much to my surprise, in just a few weeks, what was to have been a "simple shot" had mushroomed unexpectedly into a most elaborate work, taxing both my resources and my wits. For a while, I found myself broke and barefoot, in unfamiliar territory. I'd been locked into the Sleeper's pattern. It was both a great strategy and a great pitfall. *Touch and Go* had been a real turning point, but its solutions had come alarmingly late in the game.

*Touch and Go* was in place from January 7 to February 18, 1985. The case that took eight weeks to invent and build, took five minutes to state. It was dismantled a month later, gone in three hours. The bulk of the evidence was circumstantial and has disappeared. We can't touch it. Most of its parts were cannibalized, "donored" into subsequent jobs. Apart from a "wild wad" of working drawings, the only evidence left is a pair of disconnected switch boxes, slotted with the words TOUCH, GO, 3 MINS and 2 MINS.

The original testimony was a nice but yellowing review, a few left-over brochures, and a couple of sets of "slides-n-tape." Now there is this true but unlikely story of how a sound sculpture in an accessorized room was hijacked by a pattern, in plain view but off the beaten track. Closed after a month of hearings, *Touch and*

175

*Go* never got much of a trial. The evidence was entirely circumstantial. Similar cases have since been made, some in higher courts nearby. I've got a hunch the jury's still out. We're going to hear more about this.

Touch and Go

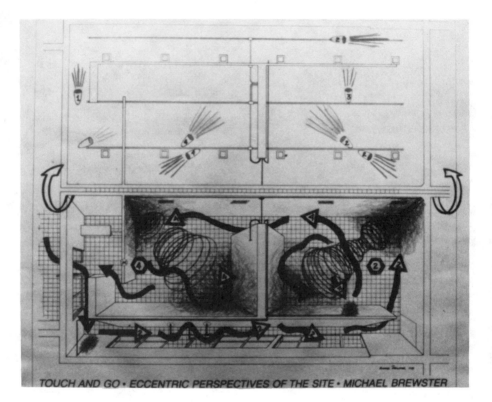

TOUCH AND GO · ECCENTRIC PERSPECTIVES OF THE SITE · MICHAEL BREWSTER

182

**Alvin Curran**

ALVIN CURRAN was born in 1938 in Providence, Rhode Island. He is considered one of the leading composer/performers in environmental and live electronic music today and his works have been performed in nearly every major new music venue in Europe and North America. He studied composition with Ron Nelson at Brown University and Elliott Carter at The Yale School of Music and in 1966 co-founded Musica Elettronica Viva with Richard Teitelbaum and Frederic Rzewski in Rome where he presently resides. In the early 1970's, Curran developed a very personal solo performance style combining his own singing, piano, synthesizers, found objects and recorded sound. His works have been performed at such institutions as Simon Fraser University (Vancouver, British Columbia), Woodland Pattern (Milwaukee, Wisconsin), The Walker Art Center (Minneapolis, Minnesota), Soundworks (Seattle, Washington), Portland Center for the Visual Arts (Portland, Oregon), The Center for Contemporary Arts (Santa Fe, New Mexico), Real Art Ways (Hartford, Connecticut), Laghetto di Villa Borghese (Rome, Italy) and the Kasseler Musiktage (Kassel, Germany). His most recent works include: *Maritime Rites*, a ten part series of environmental radio concerts performed in collaboration with John Cage, Pauline Oliveros, Malcolm Goldstein, Jon Gibson, Joseph Celli, Clark Coolidge, Leo Smith, Steve Lacy and George Lewis, and funded by National Public Radio; *Electric Rags*, a work for piano midi-interfaced with a computer and five synthesizers, and commissioned by the West Deutscher Radio, Cologne, Germany; *1985, A Piece for Peace*, a three-nation simulcast concert held on January 1, 1985 in Amsterdam, Frankfurt and Venice and recently awarded the Prix d'Italia. His works include *Natural History*, a symphonic poem based on sounds of the jungle, the desert, the forest, the tundra, underground caves, high tension wires and acoustic instruments, funded by a grant from the National Endowment for the Arts; a concert for the main square in the city of Linz; a work based on the sounds of the city of Rome, *Cartoline Romane*, commissioned by the West Deutscher Radio Horspiel Program. In February 1986 he was a composer-in-residence in West Berlin on the D.A.A.D. program. Most recently Curran has created another international radio concert involving six European countries in a simulcast in commemoration of the so called "crystal night" of November 1938. The piece is entitled "Crystal Psalms."

# Maritime Rites * The Lake

## Alvin Curran

Between 1975 and 1980 I held a student-created teaching position at the Accademia Nazionale d'Arte Drammatica in Rome. My role there was primarily to teach collective vocal improvisation and related vocal and musical experimentation. From the day to day classes, ideas and pieces began to emerge which united my own personal interests in environmental music with the specific artistic goals of the students. *The Lake*, in fact, was born of these circumstances. It was an end-of-the-year project (1978) and left me not only with the memory of a spirited performance but with the beginnings of a series of pieces called *Maritime Rites*, which since then have led me to tracking down and recording all of the fog horns on the eastern seaboard of the United States (National Public Radio grant, 1985), directing ships horn concerts in European ports, large scale river concerts (*The Rhone*, Festival d'Avignon, 1987), as well as a radio concert (*1985-A Piece for Peace*) broadcast simultaneously from churches in Venice, Frankfurt and Amsterdam - in a word, the modest beginnings of my "putting natural sound back into nature," evidenced in *The Lake* have had very important consequences for my work in general.

*The Lake* itself is really quite simple; in fact, it consists of nothing more than several small groups of people (five or six) singing in row boats while rowing aimlessly on a small quiet lake. All I have done is to adopt the basic elements of an everyday piece of music-theater and focus our attention on these elements themselves: random polyphony, chance choreography, and music in true spatial motion. The latter element gets special attention, for unlike even the most sophisticated electronic placement of sound in space, *The Lake* is an example of authentic music in motion where chords, melodies and rhythms are constantly floating from left-to-right, right-to-left, front-to-back, at times even circling the listener or disappearing around corners and reemerging elsewhere. Wherever the boats move, so does the music; their "free choreography" tends to enhance and merge with the kinds of musical gestures that each boat is responsible for.

Before I describe some of the musical details, I would like to say a word about collective vocal music. The years (1966-1972), following those of my formal musical studies at Yale (The School of Music), were spent founding and refounding the Musica Elettronica Viva group in Rome. These were times of true musical research

185

where every interesting clue and avenue that could revitalize our musical perspectives were pursued. The group's dedication to live electronics and free improvisation soon led to long debates on who is and who is not a musician, who can "sit-in" and who can't. In the end, the group, in a work called *Soundpool*, decided everyone was musician and simply invited everyone to play with us - which, of course, everyone did, effectively obliterating all distinctions between performer and public as well as between good and bad. When I began my teaching at the Accademia I drew readily from this well of recent experience and theorized roughly in the following way:

a) the human species is an exceptionally musical one

b) each individual possesses his own personal music

c) all healthy men and women possess a common and universal musical instrument - the voice

d) anyone can sing and anyone can sing his own music alone or in groups

e) therefore, make all possible musics with people singing their own personal music together.

As fragile as the logic of these propositions may seem, it was strong enough to convince most of my students that they were "instant musicians" (and this was also true of many less-likely people - housewives to provincial opera-singers - who participated in workshops that I conducted in these years). My point, in fact, was that music is not made from logic and ideas alone, and that the deep eternal mysteries of music making are really quite accessible to anyone who is willing to sing and listen seriously. So it was not the "logic" that convinced anyone, but the actual act of making sound, which for many of these "non-musicians" was like leaping into a pleasant void. The act of singing a tone and simultaneously becoming the tone you sing, and the act of becoming (disappearing into) someone else's sound was the doublefaced cornerstone of this work - in short, the making of deeply felt sound and intense listening to everyone and everything around you at the same time. Sound and silence were equals.

Elsewhere around the world, musicians and theater groups carried on a variety of collective vocal-music activities. Among them were: Pauline Oliveros (*Sonic Meditations* at the Center for Music Experiment, UCSD); Roberto Lanieri (the group "Prima Materia"); Bonnie Barnett with her nationwide radio-linked sing, *Tunnel Hum*; the Harmonica Choir of David Hykes; the mass outdoor solstice chantings of Charlie Morrow, Trevor Wishart and Maggie Nichols in England; Peter Hammel and Peter

186

Müller in Germany; not to mention the well known pioneering work done by theater groups such as that of Jerzy Grotowski, The Living Theater, the Roy Hart Theater and several Zen-oriented Japanese theater collectives.

For some, collective singing meant putting "people's music" back into the hands of the people, "tuning" (getting into harmony) with oneself and others, or a way of stepping momentarily out of reality; while for others, it was a pseudo-spiritual activity and a serious pathway toward some kind of universal experience.

As rich and varied as the practices and goals of each of the groups and individuals cited, I can safely assume that their work, like my own, was based on the search and propagation of those magical unifying moments when two or more human voices begin to sing the "same" music spontaneously. Along the way, of course, one heard humming, chanting, hissing, growling, howling, riffing, gurgling, snapping, hooting, cackling, bellowing and crooning. There was barnyard chaos and very often sublime harmonic revelation. Open-ended singing sessions often ended leaving the participants in a state of elation, but physically exhausted. But, whatever the results and whatever the methods, techniques or plans used to achieve them, I can safely say that they all depended on a few basic social agreements and fundamental attitudes:

1) complete mutual trust among performers

2) a general attempt to sublimate one's ego

3) acceptance of the basic rule of all improvised music: "when in doubt, lay out." Or, SILENCE is always the best musical choice.

Whether one group concentrated on the multiphonic techniques of the Tibetans and Mongols, or another mimicked the complexity of a Coltrane solo, or still others, in search of something completely unknown, used no guidelines whatsoever, some singing for ten minutes and some for ten hours, one would find that the three fundamental rules I've outlined above would at some point in the course of the work become evident and necessary for continued development.

I began to work with methods and techniques suitable to my own musical interest at the time (which essentially were centered on a conscious mixing of imaginary cosmic harmony with earthly anarchy). And though I did not devise any systematic curriculum or even keep track of the exercises and pieces I would invent daily, practice and time brought about a natural codification of a number of these vocal "gestures": and they became a set of repeatable improvisational and compositional structures. *The Lake* is my first large-scale piece which employs a number of them.

Here I was neither inventing anything new nor discrediting anything old; I was simply speaking a language I had recently acquired and teaching others (fifty-two young theater students, unable to read conventional music notation) how to speak it as well. The language of experimental music, largely born of the '50's and widely developed in the '60's by LaMont Young, Christian Wolff, John Cage, Cornelius Cardew and the Scratch Orchestra, Pauline Oliveros and the group Musica Elettronica Viva, was created by musicians for musicians and for "non-musicians" (non-professionals) as well; hundreds of pieces were created by giving simple instructions or game like rules to follow, or graphic signs to interpret, enabling practically anyone to participate.

The most frequently used instruction in my class-work at that time was "sing a well placed, freely chosen tone lasting one long breath." This basic vocal-structure often served as a point of departure for many exercises and gradually rose in status to be considered a genuine musical statement. Any long tone, then, became equivalent to "music." Of the many variants I used on the long tone, only an essential few are employed in *The Lake*. They are: sing long tones, for the duration of one breath, in the low, middle or high registers; sing in unison (on a tone given by the group leader); sing two or three notes contiguously on one breath; sing uninterruptedly (i.e. repeating the same tone immediately following the end of the preceding one); sing in very slow ascending or descending glissandi.

Of short tones, I used two types: the first lasting from one tenth of a second to three seconds given with conventional conducting signs by the group leader. Here the unforeseeable nature of the conductors signs keeps the performers in a high state of attention. The second short tone was periodic and of a single duration (also directed by the group leader).

In contrast to these conducted, freely chosen tones, I employed two kinds of improvisation. One encouraged a random but constant density of lyrical and melodic singing on any known or invented "song." The second type was a more disjointed, fragmentary type allowing for more individual interactions.

In addition, two other special symbols appeared which gave a very determinate character to the piece: the "M" which initiated a concerted unison melody chosen by the members of each boat, bringing a moment of motivic naturalism into the work. And the ≈ which initiated an imitation of the music sung by another

188

group in another boat. This sign had a specially determining role in the piece, for when, by pure coincidence, two boats had the "imitate" instruction at the same time, and by chance decided to imitate one another, endless loops and chain reactions were generated.

Far from being a casual free improvisation, this highly structured piece greatly depends on the instant choices made by the leader/singers in each boat. And while empowered with great responsibilities of choice and action, the very presence of ten or so conductors combined with the innate randomness of the parts they are conducting forestalls the possibility of anyone "usurping power." In fact, this piece is about no-one, hence everyone, "being in charge."

One more word about space. *The Lake*, as I mentioned earlier, was a key work in my continued interest in incorporating public spaces into my musical language and practice. While this tendency is much in vogue with festival organizers, city planners and cultural politicians, it was for me a quite natural development stemming from my long time occupation with gathering and recording all kinds of sounds - sounds that have become a stable part of my musical vocabulary. Again, my intention with *The Lake* and my subsequent pieces for open fields, plazas, facades, rooftops, entire buildings, ports, rivers and coastlines, was essentially to put natural music back into nature, and to let the physical dimensions, acoustics, appearance of and weather at these sites play a determining role in the nature of the music itself. While not as pure as, say, the phenomenological pieces of my colleague Alvin Lucier, these works fully support the central idea of his work of letting the place, thing or object BE its own music. To second Sun Ra's well known motto: "Space is the place." With no added frills or theatricality, *The Lake* is simply composed of the entire surroundings of its given site, its ambient noises and perceived rhythm of events and their natural passage of time. The musicians just happen to be there.

For an effective realization, *The Lake* requires a mixed chorus of at least fifty voices distributed five to six per boat. The five parts (A, B, C, D, E) are assigned in successive order, one per boat. This ensures a polyphony the end results of which, though foreseen, are in no way foreseeable. And while no two performances of the piece will ever be the same, the nature of the simple musical gestures and their execution provides a rather predictable overall texture whose ever-changing densities, movement through space (on the lake itself), and lapses into short or very long silences, for no apparent reason - much the way insects and birds start and stop their songs - gives this work its basic musical profile. With this in mind, an optimal performance of *The Lake* should be one which blends harmoniously with the environment in which it takes place.

Until now versions of this work have tended to last about one hour, though the score itself suggests the possibility of a piece lasting several hours. Performances, to date, have been held at: L'Estate Romana, Laghetto di Villa Borgese, Roma, Italy, 1980; Kassler Musiktage, Baggerloch, Kassel, Germany, 1981; The Walker Arts Center, Loring Pond, Minneapolis, Minnesota, USA, 1982; New Music America IV, Lake Michigan, Chicago, Illinois, USA, 1982; Fles Festival IV, Lago del Retiro, Madrid, Spain, 1983.

# - THE LAKE -

# MARITIME RITES - ALVIN CURRAN.

## requisites:

1. an appropriate group of 50-150 singers - professionals or not - who have some feeling for or experience in improvised music.

2. a number of row boats sufficient to distribute the group minimally 5-6/boat.

3. a small body of water in relatively quiet surroundings on which to float the boats.

4. a "director" to be chosen from among the members of each boat

5. one cassette-tape player/boat with audible playback

6. 5-10 conch shells distributed to not more than one player-singer/boat - note: this is an autonomous part and to be used very sparsely alone or in reply to others in free moments only.

## general notes to all participants:

the main components of this work are randomness and tranquillity - little space is given to drammatic or consequential gestures. Most sounds that occur will simply appear to have "happened" that way and for no apparent reason. So, it is important to remember: THERE IS NO NEED TO HURRY and SILENCE IS JUST AS IMPORTANT AS SOUND, LISTENING AS IMPORTANT AS SINGING

given the musical nature of this work and the ever-changing physical and acoustical situations of the singers and boats: interplay and reaction between boats will in some cases be unavoidable or desireable while in other cases independence and isolation may be favored. The conductors should pay special attention to the total sound and progress of the music at any given time and act with conscious involvement and commitment. DYNAMICS (forte, piano etc.) are therefore left to the discretion of the directors. as a consequence any combination of loud and quiet may occur at any time. Volume, then, like entries, durations, pauses, etc. is spontaneously determined.

## about the score:

1. excluding the introduction and ending each score (part) is divided into 49 events

2. the total duration of a single event (including repeats) should not last more than ca. 3 minutes and silences

3. an event may be singular          repeated          or continuous

4. events are separated one from another by pauses given in minutes          24"          1'30"
and seconds:          etc.

5. there are 5 different parts (A, B, C ...) and should be distributed evenly among the boats. e.g. Boats 1-5, score A; Boats 6-10, score B; etc...

6. the entire score is interpreted and directed by the "leader" of each boat

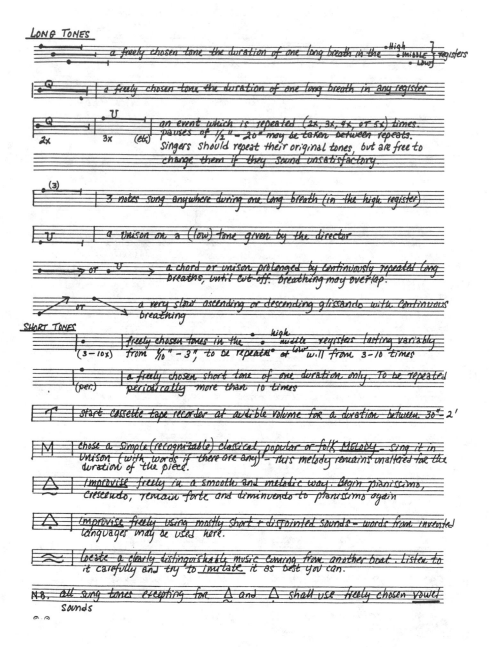

## LONG TONES

- a freely chosen tone the duration of one long breath in the {high / middle / low} registers
- a freely chosen tone the duration of one long breath in _any register_
- an event which is repeated (2x, 3x, 4x, or 5x) times. pauses of ½" – 20" may be taken between repeats. Singers should repeat their original tones, but are free to change them if they sound unsatisfactory.
- (3) 3 notes sung anywhere during one long breath (in the high register)
- a unison on a (low) tone given by the director
- or → a chord or unison prolonged by continuously repeated long breaths, until cut off. breathing may overlap.
- or → a very slow ascending or descending glissando with continuous breathing

## SHORT TONES

- (3–10x) freely chosen tones in the {high / middle / low} registers lasting variably from 1/10" – 3", to be repeated at will from 3–10 times
- (per.) a freely chosen short tone of one duration only. To be repeated periodically more than 10 times
- ↑ start cassette tape recorder at audible volume for a duration between 30" – 2'
- M chose a simple (recognizable) classical, popular or folk MELODY – sing it in unison (with words if there are any) – this melody remains unaltered for the duration of the piece.
- △ improvise freely in a smooth and melodic way. Begin pianissimo, crescendo, remain forte and diminuendo to pianissimo again
- △ improvise freely using mostly short + disjointed sounds – words from invented languages may be used here.
- ≈ locate a clearly distinguishable music coming from another boat. Listen to it carefully and try to _imitate_ it as best you can.

N.B. all sung tones excepting for △ and △ shall use freely chosen _vowel_ sounds

# A

intro
while boarding boats
Unison
3' while embarking
3'
continue U with gradual modulations
ending
all the boats converge at one point and the singers
improvise a steady and increasingly exuberant crescendo
for 5 min. ca. cutoff on cue.

B

intro | while boarding | while embarking | 5ea.

Unison → | continue 1ˢᵗ with gradual modulations →

(3 - 10x)

ending

all the boats converge at one point and the singers improvise in long and exuberant crescendo which remains "forte" for 5 min. ea. until cutoff.

# C

195

Maritime Rites/The Lake - New Music America IV, Chicago, July '82

**Thomas DeLio**

THOMAS DELIO was born in 1951 in New York City. He is a composer and theorist. He studied at the New England Conservatory of Music in Boston and Brown University in Providence, Rhode Island where he received a Ph.D. in an interdisciplinary studies program combining mathematics, music and the visual arts. His articles on the music of Luigi Dallapiccola, Elliott Carter, Iannis Xenakis, John Cage, Philip Glass, Robert Ashley, Morton Feldman and Alvin Lucier, among others, have appeared in *The Musical Quarterly, Perspectives of New Music, The Journal of Music Theory, Artforum, Interface, Sonus, Indiana Theory Review, Percussive Notes, Brass Bulletin* and *Winds Quarterly*. He is the author of two books on contemporary music: *Circumscribing the Open Universe* (University Press of America, 1984); and, *Contiguous Lines: Issues and Ideas in the Music of the '60's and '70's* (University Press of America, 1985). He is co-editor, with Dr. Stuart Smith, of *Twentieth Century Music Scores* (Prentice-Hall, 1989). In addition, he is currently working on a book entitled *The Music of Morton Feldman* (Excelsior Press, forthcoming). As a composer, Thomas DeLio has distinguished himself in the area of computer aided composition and as the creator of a series of live electronic sound installations. His works are published by Smith Publications/Sonic Art Editions of Baltimore, Maryland. A number of compositions are recorded on the Spectrum label: *Serenade* (SR-128, 1980); *Marginal Developments* (SR-144, 1982); *Gestures* (SR-163, 1982); and, *Partial Manifolds* (SR-302, 1985). Also, two works are forthcoming on compact discs: *Against the silence ...* (Wergo) and *Text* (Mode). Thomas DeLio's installations have been exhibited in such institutions as the Baltimore Museum of Art and the Corcoran Gallery of Art in Washington, D.C. Articles about his work have appeared in *Leonardo, Interface* and *Percussive Notes*. He has received grants from Meet the Composer, The Ludwig Vogelstein Foundation and The University of Maryland. Thomas DeLio has taught at Clark University in Worcester, Massachusetts and The New England Conservatory of Music in Boston, Massachusetts. He is currently an Associate Professor in the Department of Music of the University of Maryland at College Park.

# Installation: Strathmore Hall Arts Center, 1985

## Thomas DeLio

Toward the end of his last book, *Mr. Palomar*, Calvino contemplates his perspicacious character's ability to sense and, in turn, be sensed in the world:

> And what about him, also known as "I," namely Mr.
> Palomar? Is he not a piece of the world that is looking
> at another piece of the world? Or else, given that
> there is world that side of the window and world this
> side, perhaps the "I," the ego, is simply the window
> through which the world looks at the world. To look
> at itself the world needs the eyes (and the eyeglasses)
> of Mr. Palomar.[1]

Through this eloquent synthesis, Calvino, echoing Wittgenstein and many others, determines that what we understand about the world is rooted in the way we perceive the world. Through the act of perception, Mr. Palomar discovers that his presence constitutes the nexus of all the forces which form his understanding of reality. Through his presence, he gives meaning to every event on his horizon. Calvino and Palomar are, of course, one and the same. Palomar's eyes and eyeglasses are those of Calvino who, through his creation, reaches for the impossibility of separating himself - for even one moment - from his perceptions, only to find himself inevitably drawn in at the moment of each perception.

The most exciting art of our time strives for some tangible representation of those acts which define experience: the reciprocal forces of perception and consciousness. Toward this same goal, for the past seven years I have been working on a series of electronic sound installations designed to interact with the various architectural properties of their respective sites. Through the introduction of subtle sound combinations, as well as occasional visual elements, all carefully placed throughout the space, I attempt to bind site and perceiver together, heightening the perceiver's awareness of the locus of his experience. As do a number of recent visual artists such as Robert Irwin and Carl Andre, and several composers, most notably Alvin Lucier and Max Neuhaus, through my installations I attempt to focus the perceiver upon the site of his experience - the frame which surrounds all experience and from which all meaning arises.

In fashioning each installation, I attempt to draw its structure from that of the environment in which the work is perceived rather than from any abstract notion of design; "place," then, becomes "structure." Toward this end, I have found it necessary to move music out of its traditional performance environment and, simultaneously, to strip it of all the rhetoric (dramatic, gestural, linear) which was born of and is still nurtured by that medium. Typically, I introduce a few barely perceptible elements (sonic and/or visual) into a space. These act as invisible bonds uniting perceiver with site, leading him toward a new awareness of the site and of the ways in which space appears to change as he moves through and around it.

In this shift from abstraction to site, I hope to engage the perceiver in new ways and challenge the belief that, in experience, there is an ideal, "geometric" congruence between idea and object. Emphasis is placed upon presence: The simultaneous presence of oneself and the locus of one's experience. As the perceiver becomes conscious of the site, he becomes conscious of his presence as the focus of that site for himself. The perceiver and the perceived define each other as contradictory, yet inseparable boundaries, each drawing the other into consciousness simultaneously. In my installations, the site becomes the ground upon which this reciprocal action occurs. For me, these works are an expression of the reality that "place" is the focal point between each individual and the world around him.

I have presented a number of different installations since 1978 at such institutions as The Baltimore Museum of Art and The Corcoran Gallery in Washington, D.C.[2] The Work which I will discuss in this paper is untitled and was created for the Strathmore Hall Arts Center in Rockville, Maryland (see diagrams following this essay). It was installed at this site from March 9 through 17, 1985.

The Center is located in a spacious 19th century mansion in which rooms on both the first and second floors are used to display artworks. I used the entire first floor. In particular, I was drawn to the rather fragmented experience of space which I had when walking around this first floor. I was struck by the fact that, aside from perhaps the central hallway, no matter which room I happened to be in I tended to feel isolated and cut off from the rest of the site and found it difficult to locate myself within the entire space of the building. One of my goals, then, became the experiential unification of this fragmented environment. This presented a challenge quite different from that posed by any other space in which I had previously worked, where the site had always been extremely well integrated and my contribution tended either to enhance or play against this internal coherence.

The perceptual integration of Strathmore Hall was achieved through the use of two extremely different materials - one sonic and the other visual. These led the perceiver to draw the space together in his mind. The visual component of the piece consisted of a single, very thin thread of transparent monofilament stretched in an unbroken straight line through the entire length of the mansion - front to back - at a height of approximately seven feet from the ground. This line was drawn through the foyer and central hallway of the first floor (which follow one another consecutively) and divided these spaces asymmetrically (once again, see diagrams following essay). Due to the nature of this monofilament - its extreme thinness and near transparence - it was always just barely visible and at times, as the light changed or as one shifted one's vantage point, it even seemed to disappear. In general, the line was not visible from a distance of more than five or six feet and, more important, was never visible from any room other than the ones in which it was hung. Finally, of great significance was the fact that, due to its length, one could never see all of it at once. If one stood still and attempted to visually trace the line along its entire length, it always seemed to disappear into space.

The sonic component of the piece consisted of one square wave filtered to almost sine tone purity (fundamental frequency 466Hz, Bb4), played continuously and quite softly. This particular sound was chosen because it was especially resonant in the space in which it was heard, one of the small side rooms just off the main hallway. Though very soft, it could be perceived from any point in this room; however, it was inaudible from any other room in the building. The electronic equipment used to produce this tone is described fully in the documentation following this essay. Basically, a signal from a square wave oscillator was routed through a low pass filter. It was played through a special, high quality, miniature speaker (2 3/4" x 2 3/4" x 3 1/2") which was discreetly placed in a corner of the room, near the ceiling and covered with material which blended into the environment. All wires and electronic equipment (oscillator, amplifier, filter etc.) were hidden from view. As such, the tone appeared to simply hover in the room with no apparent point of origin.

As one experienced the piece, these two components tended to complement one another. The line united the space from end to end. Since it was never itself entirely visible from any one location, the viewer was drawn to move along it and discover its limits - the limits of the building. In addition, this line cut the space of the central rooms of the mansion asymmetrically leading the viewer to reintegrate those spaces as he constantly attempted to focus upon the monofilament, locate its position in space and orient himself to it. In contrast, the sound appeared to fill one entire room. It was perceived as a material filling a specific volume of space. The room itself, then, appeared to function rather like a container. By extension, each room took on a similar quality and the entire building seemed no longer an agglomeration of random spaces but rather a body of irregularly shaped containers - one filled, the others empty. This gave each room a more object-like quality than is usually associated with such spaces, especially those in a museum where rooms are used for the display of art works and are not in themselves the center of our attention.

Together, these two dispirate sonic and visual ideas balanced one another: one cut through space while the other filled it; one led the viewer to join different spaces, removing the internal partitions of rooms within the building, while the other led him to conceive each room as a distinct and separate object. Each element led to very different, almost contradictory, conceptions of space. Faced with this, the viewer was, I hope, led to focus more intensely upon just what constituted the experience of this particular site.

In addition to the issues of presence and perception which, as discussed earlier, are of paramount importance to this and other installations which I have created, several other related issues arise. The first involves the notion of impermanence. Each installation exists only for the duration of its presentation at the site (usually imposed by outside forces - gallery directors and museum schedules). It cannot be written down in the manner of a more traditional piece of music and then transported to any number of different locations and performed over again. Each is wedded to its site and would make no sense if somehow perceived apart from that specific site. This rather fragile temporality leads one to focus upon the moment, with no experience of past or future tied to it. Thus, through these installations, I strive for an expression without memory; not an expression "of something" but a "presence" to be experienced anew each time.

Another significant issue is the creation of a non-performance art. In the recent twentieth century, significant transformations have taken place in and among the various media in this regard. In the visual arts, one today finds a flourishing group of practitioners of what is known as "performance art"; while, in music, one finds some composers trying, in various ways, to step out of the world of performance - which has so dominated this medium throughout history - in order to

202

create an entirely new mode of expression. In my sound installations, I strive for a musical experience which eschews all vestige of performance and theater and is, therefore, perhaps more closely allied to the traditional world of the visual arts. In them, I try to create a situation in which the listener and his relationship to the space around him are of paramount importance. My specific purpose is to make the perceiver more conscious of his experience by focusing on the framework of that experience (the site) and, ultimately, to make that framework the very subject of experience itself.

1. Italo Calvino, *Mr. Palomar* (New York: Harcourt, Brace and Jovanovich Publishers, 1985), p. 114.

2. Michael Hamman, "Toward a Morphology of Presence: The Sound Installations of Thomas DeLio," *Interface*, (Vol. 16, Nos. 1-2), pp. 55-73; Errata (Vol. 16, No. 4).

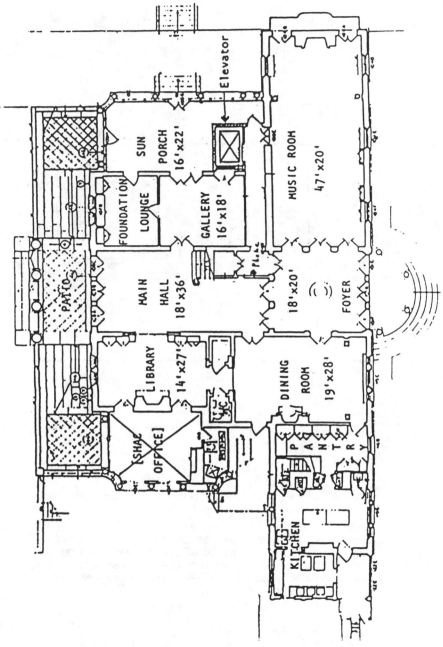

Strathmore Hall; first floor

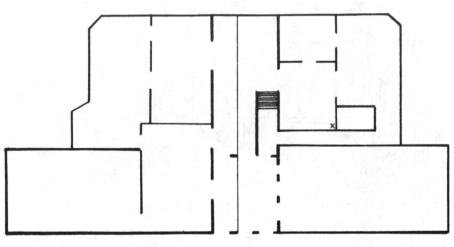

⊢6'⊣⊢12'⊣

_____ = one piece of very thin, barely visible monofilament, stretched taught approximately seven feet above the floor.

    X = miniature speaker (2 3/4"x 2 3/4"x 3 1/2") placed unobtrusively in corner, near ceiling; all wires and sound equipment hidden from view. The sound employed consisted of one, extremely soft square wave (fundamental frequency, 466 Hz - Bb4), filtered to almost sine tone purity (audible throughout the room in which the speaker was placed but inaudible from any other room).

## Equipment

| | |
|---|---|
| *Speaker* | Micro Fidelity MFS-6300<br>3 1/2" x 2 3/4" x 2 3/4"<br>200-20,000Hz |
| *Oscillator* | Southwest Technical Products Corp.<br>Top Octave Generator |
| *Divider* | Southwest Technical Products Corp.<br>Seven Stage Binary Divider |
| *Filter* | Filter bank with low/high pass filters |

The pitch generator divides a 2-240MHz reference frequency 13 ways to generate 13 tones of the top octave C7 through C8 (2093.01 to 4186.02Hz). These divisions approximate the equally tempered scale. The divider module takes any four of these tones and generates all equivalent lower octave notes down to zero. If, for example, one input of one divider module is fed note A7, the outputs of the module will be eight tones (A7 down to A0), each precisely one octave (2:1) lower in pitch. Each output may be either a square or sawtooth wave and may be filtered to a sine or near sine wave through a filter bank.

**Ron Kuivila**

RON KUIVILA was born in 1955 in Boston, Massachusetts. He is a composer and artist. He studied at Wesleyan University and Mills College where he received a MFA in composition. His work has focused primarily on live electronic music and interactive sound installations. These pieces frequently involve the use of unusual home-made or home-modified equipment. He has performed throughout North America and Europe in concert halls such as the Kitchen (New York City) and De Ijsbreker (Amsterdam) and at festivals such as New Music America. His sound installations have been exhibited by the San Francisco Art Institute, The Brattleboro Art Museum and The Piezoelectric Gallery in New York, among others.

Kuivila has collaborated with a number of other artists, composers and choreographers including Rudy Burchardt, Nicolas Collins, Merce Cunningham, Douglas Dunn, Susan Foster, Larry Polansky, Mel Wong and Paul Zelevansky. He has also collaborated with David Anderson, a computer scientist, on the development of a real time computer music system called FORMULA. His music is recorded on the Lovely Music/Vital Records label and also may be found in both the Tellus and Slowscan cassette magazines.

# Sound Installations

## Ron Kuivila

*A little background*

For a composer, sound installations create a relationship to audiences drastically different from that of the concert hall. People gather together at a scheduled time to sit and listen for a concert. An installation is a more anarchic venue. People are free to come and go as they please, changing their position relative to the sounds they hear and sights they see. This freedom can serve to enable a different conception of sound. In a good concert hall sound acts as the ethereal conveyance of music; it brings the same music to everyone and perhaps brings them together in the process. The physicality of sound, subdued by good acoustical design, is ignored. The gallery situation makes possible a more physical encounter with sound as a phenomenon with sculptural properties. The spatial formations of sound created in Alvin Lucier's standing wave installations provide a striking example. David Tudor's *Rainforest IV* is more concerned with the physicality of sound production. It is a concert piece forced into the gallery by the conflict between its creative intent and the conventions of the concert hall. As such, it can characterize some of the issues I would like to discuss.

In *Rainforest*, found objects, selected for their sonic interest, are transformed into loudspeakers capable of amplifying and (more importantly) transforming sound. These objects comprise a varied collection of carefully made "low fidelity" speakers with complex filtering and spatial characteristics. (This project is not as unfamiliar as it my seem; we do not prize the violin because it perfectly amplifies the noisy ramp wave generated by dragging a bow across a string.) The piece can be seen as a collection of musical in instruments that prize idiosyncracy over regularity. Each speaker is unique, equally interesting as an object and as a producer of sound. For a performance, the speakers are distributed throughout the concert hall or gallery. There is no formal audience seating. People wander amongst the objects, encountering them both as individual objects making individual sounds and as constituents of a larger forest of sound. The piece is realized by a group of composer/performers who select objects and provide them with sound. (The score provides the technical information needed to do this, little more). From the perspective of the concert tradition, this is a music that empowers the audience, the musicians, and even their instruments to act for themselves. This cannot be easily accommodated by the monarchy of the concert hall. Tactically, the work almost demands to be presented as an installation.

The ongoing nature of a gallery installation gives rise to a small, shifting audience. This makes it possible to make works that people can 'interact' with in a more concrete, causal way than can happen in the walkthrough situation of a *Rainforest* performance. If this interaction is to be self-conscious, the piece must gracefully handle performers of unknown skills. Robert Rauschenberg's *Soundings* is a particulary elegant example. It consists of a one way mirror that hides an elaborate construction hanging chairs from view. Sounds made in the gallery turn on lights that illuminate the space behind the mirror revealing the construction hiding there (a collection of hanging chairs). Spectators quickly recognize their role and begin to "play" the installation.

These soundings do more than reveal Rauschenberg's chairs. The whistling, loud talking, and even yelling it encourages are serious breaches of gallery etiquette. These demonstrations call attention to the conventions of the gallery and the social power they assume. Happily, the demonstrations do not turn into a riot. People's responses to the piece may annoy or amuse, but the visual imprint they generate is always interesting. The details of peoples's actions are limited to the social and auditory environment of the piece; any sound whatsoever generates a winning visual image. The sculpture accommodates performance by limiting its scope.

*Installations with ultrasound*

Much of my work has involved the creation of sound fields that are sensitive to movement. In these pieces, people directly confront the physicality of sound, but in so doing, they become performers. Thus the pieces share some of the concerns I have attributed to *Rainforest* and *Soundings*.

These installations transpose ultrasound, sound above the range of human hearing, into audible sound. This transposition has the effect of revealing properties of sound that are normally too subtle to perceive. The transposition technique takes sounds ranging from 30,000 hertz to 50,000 hertz (an interval of a major sixth, well above human hearing) and transforms them into sounds between 1 to 20,000 hertz (more than ten octaves). So pitches within an interval of less than an octave are augmented to a range larger than we can hear.

Any time something moves, any sound that happens to bounce off the mover is shifted slightly in pitch. This doppler shift is normally too small to be heard. The expansion of pitch intervals just described makes this phenomenon fully audible. Ultrasound is more easily affected by air currents and changes in temperature and humidity. The sound retains this imprint as it is transposed, bringing it within hearing. This has been extended to allow the flickering of a flame to be translated into audible sound. The installations have explored these properties, the relationships of sound and movement they engender, and the social situations they create as "interactive" musical situations.

The first installations I made with ultrasound were very simple. Oscillators were distributed through the gallery together with transposing microphones, amplifiers, and speakers. The oscillators were arranged and tuned to create tone clusters whose mixture would shift with air currents and people's movements, a cloud of sound that trembled in the breeze. Motion also produced a low airy rumble whose pitch was determined by the speed of movement. I always viewed this as a side effect, analogous to fallen leaves one can walk through quietly or noisily. My chief concern was the generalization of this tremulous cloud of sound. Many visitors of these pieces did not share that attitude; the simple fact that they could elicit a direct, audible response overpowered all else. The instrumental connection people had with these pieces overwhelmed all other considerations. This could be quite interesting when an inventive visitor explored the situation. But, more often than not, dull and even aggressive behavior was the result. I was happy to open these pieces to the creativity of others, but I felt that I must take responsibility for the unfortunate situations that sometimes resulted. These considerations were foremost when I made *Untitled*.

In *Untitled* I tried to design an installation that would encourage careful performances and fail to respond to inattentive or aggressive actions. The sounds generated by people's movements were passed to a microcomputer where they were processed. The interposition of the computer made it possible to tailor the response of the installation. The motion-sensing was made most sensitive to slow, steady movements that practically anyone can execute gracefully while continuing to listen. Harmonic changes were triggered by the absence of movement. Thus, the decision to stop and listen elicited a change in the system's behavior. The computer actually filtered the movement generated sounds and transposed the filtered sound into sixteen distinct harmonizations. Visitors literally moved through a sound world composed for them.

I extended these considerations to the visual setting of the piece. The room was illuminated with a single light source directed just in front of the area where the installation was most sensitive to movement. There, it illuminated a barrier of broken glass that blocked people from entering too far into the region. All of the illumination of the room came from the tattered reflections of the light off the glass. In order to play the installation, one had to approach the glass. This resulted in almost completely eliminating all illumination. This drastic and somewhat unexpected loss of light combined with the implied threat of the broken glass to create a situation that encouraged cautions actions.

Confronted with an unfamiliar situation, people seem to first analyze it "instrumentally." In an interactive installation, a person's causal connection to the piece can eliminate any other considerations. *Untitled* was an attempt to make a piece that explored the fascination of instrumental connection without being overwhelmed by it.

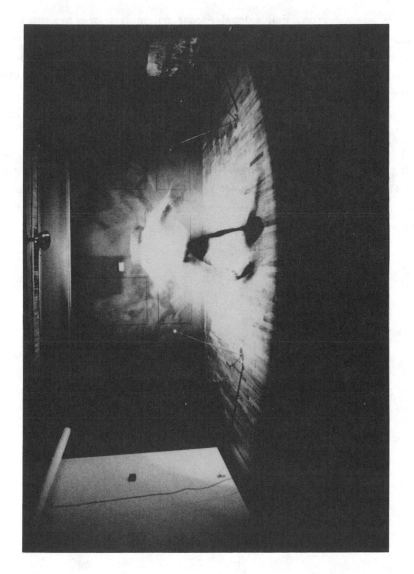

Untitled

A schematic for a simple doppler sonar motion detector is presented on the next page. The circuit functions by broadcasting a single 40,000 hertz tone throughout an area. People, and most objects, create reflections of this tone. Movement causes these reflections to experience a small change in pitch termed doppler shift. The mixture of different reflections with different amounts of doppler shift creates audible frequency beating patterns. The circuitry presented here detects those beating patterns and "decodes" them into an audible signal.

Additional oscillators at slightly different frequencies will create steady beating patterns that decode to steady tones. For example, a second oscillator at 40,440 hertz will decode to an "A" at 440 hertz. If the oscillators are placed rather far apart, the resultant tones will vary in volume and timbre with air currents and passers-by.

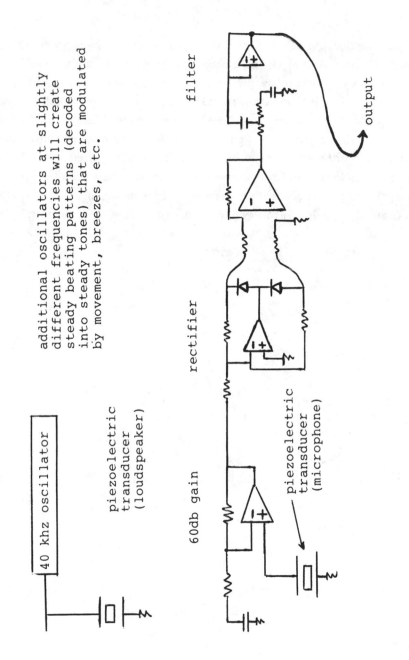

additional oscillators at slightly
different frequencies will create
steady beating patterns (decoded
into steady tones) that are modulated
by movement, breezes, etc.

40 khz oscillator

piezoelectric
transducer
(loudspeaker)

filter

rectifier

60db gain

piezoelectric
transducer
(microphone)

output

*Appendix B*
Untitled: Flow Chart


In *Untitled*, the sounds that result from ultrasound motion detection are processed digitally. This allows the apparent sensitivity of the motion sensing to be heightened and allows the interactive behavior of the system to undergo changes of character. The sound is digitized and passed through a "comb filter" which eliminates pitches that do not fall within a specified harmonic series. The algorithm for this filter is quite simple and is listed on the next page. The output of this filter is transposed upwards several octaves by a simple digital synthesizer. Two channels consisting of up to eight distinct harmonizations can be audible at any one time. A control program derives patterns of harmonization from the output of the comb filter, using frequency, amplitude and waveform to determine tone color, tempo and pitch.

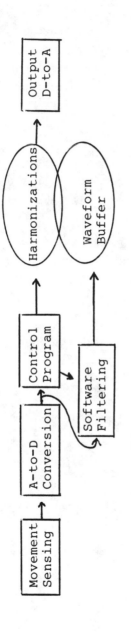

The Filtering Algorithm

on interrupt:
```
SAMPLE (I) = ((1-Q) * INPUT) + (Q * SAMPLE)
OUTPUT = SAMPLE (I)
I = (I + 1) MOD 256
RETURN
```

$Q = 7/8$

**Alvin Lucier**

ALVIN LUCIER was born in 1931 in Nashua, New Hampshire. He was educated in Nashua parochial and public schools, The Portsmouth Abbey School, Yale and Brandeis, and spent two years in Rome on a Fulbright scholarship. From 1962 to 1969 he taught at Brandeis where he conducted the Brandeis University Chamber Chorus which devoted much of its time to the performance of new mucic. In 1966 he co-founded the Sonic Arts Union with composers Robert Ashley, David Behrman and Gordon Mumma and from 1972 to 1977 was Music Director of the Viola Farber Dance Company. Since 1970 he has taught at Wesleyan University.

Lucier performs and lectures extensively and regularly contributes writings to books and periodicals. In 1984 he made a three-month concert and lecture tour of Hawaii, New Zealand, Australia and Indonesia and in the spring of 1985 he participated in a major retrospective of his work in Holland, including installations, concerts and lectures in several cities as well as an all-day radio broadcast on VPRO. His book, *Chambers*, written in collaboration with Douglas Simon, is published by the Wesleyan University Press. In addition, several of his works are available on Cramps (Italy), Mainstream, CBS Odyssey and Lovely Music records.

Lucier has been a pioneer in many areas of music composition and performance, including the notation of the performer's physical gestures, the use of brain waves in live performance, the generation of visual imagery by sound in vibrating media, and the evocation of room acoustics for musical purposes. His recent works include a series of sound installations and works for solo instruments, chamber ensembles, and orchestra in which, by means of close tunings with pure tones, sound waves are caused to spin through space.

Lucier's recent work includes two sound installations: *Seesaw*, first exhibited at The Whitney Museum of American Art in New York, Winter 1983-84; and *Spinner*, commissioned by Real Art Ways for permanent placement in Hartford, Connecticut. His orchestral work, *Crossings*, first performed by the Chicago Symphony, was given its New York premiere by the Brooklyn Philharmonic in January, 1984. He is currently working on a sound installation for the Islip Art Museum, Islip, New York, a chamber work for the New World Music Consort at Wesleyan University and a work for large orchestra.

Alvin Lucier has been the recipient of three composers grants from the National Endowment for the Arts. His *Serenade for Thirteen Winds and Pure Wave Oscillators* (1985) was commissioned by the Fromm Music Foundation.

# Seesaw

## a sound installation

### Alvin Lucier

For several years I have been exploring ways of moving sounds in space. In performance works such as *Vespers* (1968) and *Reflections of Sounds From The Wall* (1982), sound waves bounce off reflective surfaces to various points in a room. In *Directions of Sounds From The Bridge* (1979) and *The Shapes of Sounds From the Board* (1980), they flow out of musical instruments in different directions for different pitches. In *Still and Moving Lines of Silence in Families of Hyperboles* (1972-) and more recently, in *Crossings* (1982-84) and *In Memoriam John Higgins* (1985), singers and instrumental players cause ripples of sound to whirl around the concert hall. In none of these works is the movement produced by electronic switching or panning; instead, the natural characteristics of sound waves are allowed to reveal themselves.

The nature of sound waves is such that their physical presence is perceptible. In the same way that nodes and antinodes can be seen vibrating on a bowed string, crests and troughs of loud and soft sound can be perceived at regular intervals in any relatively echo-free room through which sound waves flow. The distance between crests and troughs is determined by the size of the wavelength of the sound. Low sounds have long wavelengths, up to several feet; high sounds, as small as a few inches. A at 440 cycles per seconds, for example, has a wavelength of 2.75 feet, crest to crest; C at 4186 cycles per seconds, the highest note on the piano, is about 2.5 inches long.

Because musical tones are usually complex waveforms, consisting of a fundamental and a series of overtones, their three-dimensional characteristics are virtually impossible to detect. On the other hand, pure waves, having no overtones, can be perceived as occupying physical space. One can easily discover and walk in the valley of longer wavelengths or move one's head from side to side across the crests of shorter ones. In Part III of *Still and Moving Lines*, for example, dancers are given the task of finding and walking in valleys of quiet sound created by pure waves flowing from pairs of loudspeakers. And in Part II of the same work, a singer tunes closely to two rapidly beating waves, moving her head slightly into crests of loudness in order to hear each pure wave as clearly as possible.

223

When one pure wave flows from two sources, or one source and a reflective surface, at certain points in the room the waves or their reflections collide with one another. (Because the same wave flows from two loudspeakers, one of them could be considered a reflection of another.) Where they collide in phase with each other (constructive interference), standing waves--pileups of sound as one or more waves occupy the same space--are created. Where they meet out of phase (destructive interference), they tend to cancel each other out. Because constructive or destructive interference occurs at points where a wave or multiples of that wave collide, the distances between them and their points of origin remain constant. Therefore, they form hyperbolic curves which spread out symmetrically on either side of an imaginary line between the sources. The higher the frequency of the wave, the more in number and more closely spaced the curves. For example, if two sources are 8 feet apart and the wavelength of the sound wave is 4 feet, 4 hyperbolas will form between the sources, 2 feet apart.

When two or more closely tuned musical tones are sounded, audible beats-- bumps of loud sound produced as the sound waves coincide--occur at speeds determined by the difference between the pitches of the tones. The larger the difference, the faster the beating. At unison, no beating occurs. Moreover, when two closely tuned pure tones are sounded and originate from separate loudspeakers, their physical shapes occupy nearly the same space in the room. As they beat against each other, they spin in elliptical patterns across the space, in an effort to stabilize their positions or establish primacy. As in the audible beat phenomenon, the speed of the spinning is directly related to the tuning. A difference of 1 cycle per second in produces a 1-second spin; at unison, no spinning occurs. Furthermore, since the higher wave from the one loudspeaker is oscillating faster than the other, the movement of the waves is from the higher speaker to the lower.

There is another way to imagine this . If, when the pitches in two speakers are exactly in tune with one another and you walk from one to the other, you will cross the hyperbolic paths. But as you walk from one speaker to another, a slight Doppler shift will raise the pitch of the speaker toward which you are walking and lower the pitch of the speaker from which you are receding. As the hyperbolas pass behind you, they will seem to move from the higher speaker to the lower one. Again, if one speaker is slightly higher and you walk from that speaker to the other at just the right speed, ie., the exact speed of the movement of the hyperbolas, the Doppler

224

shift will bring them into tune and you will not perceive any beating. You will be waking in sync with moving hyperbolas.

*Seesaw* is an installed work which explores the motions of two pure waves flowing from loudspeakers in an acoustically prepared room. It was first exhibited in the Film and Video Room of the Whitney Museum of American Art in New York from December 21, 1983, to January 18, 1984. The room was 38 feet long and 30 feet wide. Thirty-two 4-foot square Sonex sound-absorbing acoustical panels were mounted on the walls at regular intervals, making each room virtually echo-free. Two DCM Time Window loudspeakers were mounted facing each other on two 5-foot high pedestals in two corners of the room. The oscillators were routed through amplifiers to the loudspeakers. The complete sound system, including oscillators, amplifiers, and related equipment, was set up in an adjacent projection room, manned continuously by a technician, unseen by visitors.

The pure waves were generated by a pair of oscillators designed and built by Bob Bielecki: a crystal reference oscillator tuned to a specific frequency and a digital oscillator capable of a smooth, continuous sweep throughout the audio range. The frequency of the reference oscillator was fixed at 256 cycles per second; the other was set to sweep from 255.8 to 256.2 cycles per second, slightly below to slightly above the reference frequency. At the outer and lower limits the audible beats and spinning motions would occur once every five seconds. (Two tenths equals a fifth of cycle.) If the sweep frequency starts at unison with the fixed frequency, at 256 cycles per second, and descends toward 255.8 cps, the spinning accelerates from zero to once every 5 seconds, moving away from the reference speaker. When it reaches the lower limit the sweep then changes direction and the spinning decelerates to zero as the frequency climbs to unison again. As the sweep frequency crosses the reference frequency, rising toward the upper limit, the direction of the spinning reverses itself, moving toward the reference speaker, and the spinning speeds up again. This gesture is repeated continuously throughout the duration of the installation.

The speed of the sweep was set at a slow enough rate so that the changes of pitch were imperceptible as such and therefore would not detract from the apprehension of the physical movement of the sound waves. The length of the entire cycle-- from unison to nadir, up past unison to apex and back down to unison again-- was roughly three minutes, short enough so that even a casual visitor to the room could experience a whole cycle of movement and its reversal of direction.

The following six computer graphics by David Feldman show the combined intensity of two waves which are in tune at various phases--0, 60 120, 180, 240, 300 degrees. As the phase changes, the ridges of the contours, which represent the hyperbolic crests, may be seen to move from left to right. Each graphic represents an approximate, static visualization of the dynamic situation when one frequency is slightly higher than another.

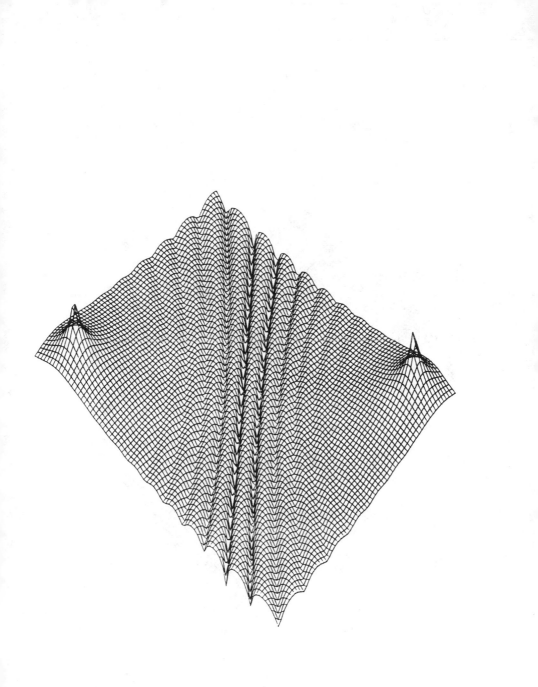

227

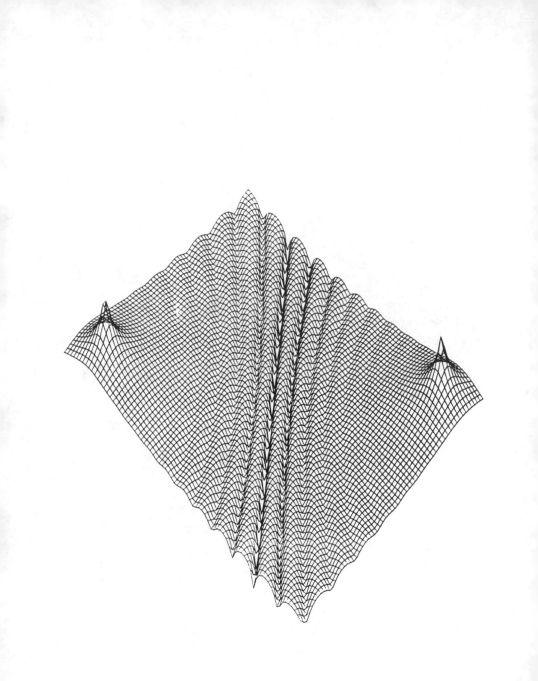

228

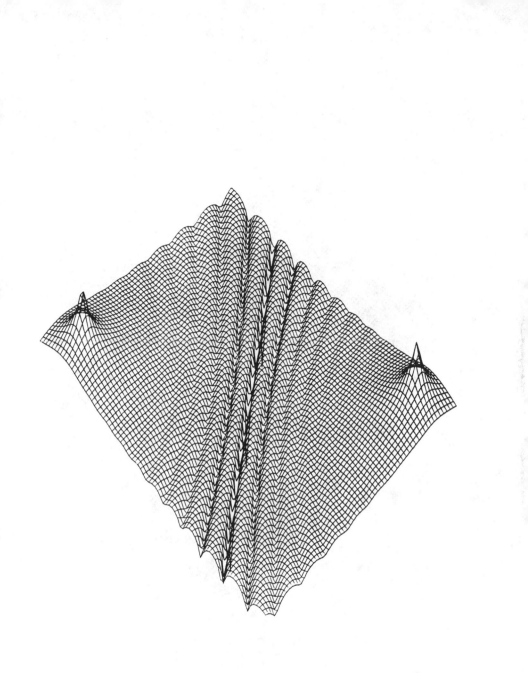

229

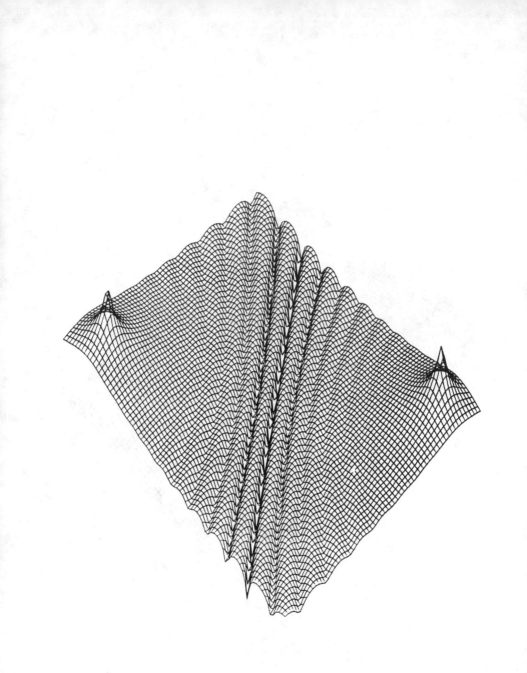

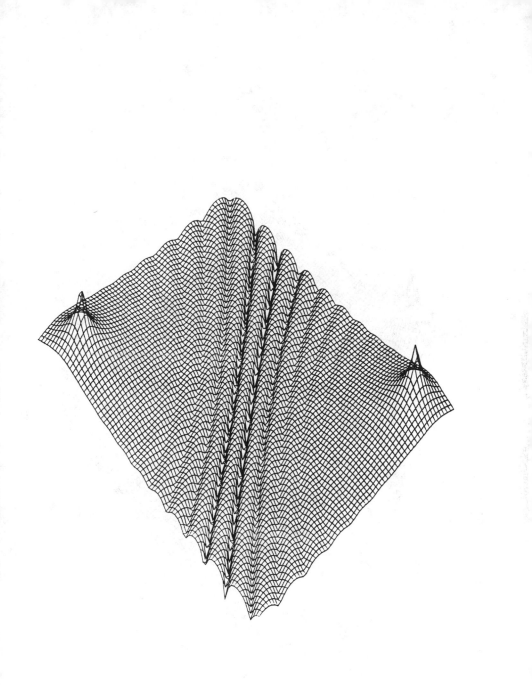

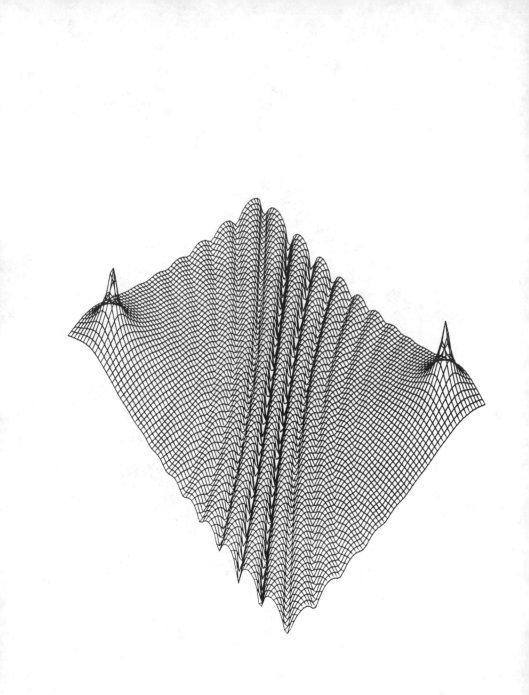

232

Max Neuhaus

MAX NEUHAUS was born in 1939 in Beaumont, Texas. He studied percussion with Paul Price at the Manhattan School of Music and became a renowned exponent of contemporary percussion music, performing as a percussion soloist on concert tours throughout the United States with Pierre Boulez (1962-63) and Karlheinz Stockhausen (1963-64). In 1964-1965 he presented solo recitals in Carnegie Hall, in New York City. His work as a percussionist culminated in an album of contemporary percussion repertoire which he recorded for Columbia Masterworks in 1968.

From the mid-1960's on, however, he began to focus more on composition and, specifically on the creation of a unique series of sound installations. Over the next two decades he created a number of outstanding works for various environments including permanent works in the United States (Times Square, New York City and the Museum of Contemporary Art, Chicago) and Europe (Villa Celle, Pistoia, Iraly and Domaine de Kerguehennec, Locmine, France) along with numerous short-term works in museums (Museum of Modern Art, the Whitney Museum of American Art, The Clocktower in New York City, ARC, Musee d'Art Moderne de la Ville de Paris, Centre National d'Art Contemporain de Grenoble in France and the Kunsthalle Basel, Switzerland).

Typically, in his works, Max Neuhaus extends the aural character of an existing space, making the perceiver more intensely aware of the natural sonic characteristics of that environment than he might otherwise be. He has worked with outdoor, indoor and underwater sites and has been equally successful in transforming each of these very different types of environments.

In support of his work, Max Neuhaus has been awarded fellowships by The Rockefeller Foundation, The Martha Baird Rockefeller Fund for Music, the National Endowment for the Arts and the Deutscher Akademischer Austauschdienst. Currently he resides in both New York and Paris.

## Max Neuhaus - Sound Installations, Techniques and Processes

### The Work For The Bell Gallery At Brown University, With Asides and Allusions

Max Neuhaus

Although most people aren't aware of it, sound is as important an aspect of how we perceive a place as the way it looks. We of course sense the size of a space with our ears as well as our eyes and our sense of position and motion may come from aural as well as visual cues. Perhaps more interesting than these psychoacoustic phenomena though, is that the feeling of the basic nature of a place and ourselves within it is determined as much by the sound as sight.

Many of these installations have been in public places, on the street or as part of transportation systems. I am always surprised when people ask me why I am interested in working in such places; as if these places were somehow unworthy of serious aesthetic endeavors. The idea being, I suppose, that unless we carefully prepare and maintain special places like museums and concert halls, and educate audiences in how to perceive works of art within them, the aesthetic experience can not occur.

I feel the opposite; i.e. that the aesthetic experience is natural to the human being, a phenomenon of living, and further that it is highly unique to each individual. By limiting it to one singular approach or particular kind of place, we have codified and classified it to the point where we begin to endanger the possibility of its occurrence.

The impetus for the first sound installation was an interest in working with a public at large, and inserting works into their daily domain in such a way that people could find them in their own time and on their own terms. Disguising them within their environments in such a way that people discovered them for themselves and took possession of them -- lead by their curiosity into listening.

Working in the context of a museum or gallery like the one for the Bell Gallery at Browns University is always a challenge -- I have to find a way or restoring the space to its natural state as a room. The starting point for each work is the space itself -- the sound which already exists there, the nature of it's acoustic and it's social context.

My first step in making a work is usually to define the sound sources or the way sound enters space. I have always found the loudspeaker to be a rather uninteresting sound source. I use it simply as a transducer; a means of translating the sound from electrical to acoustic form. Rather than using sound directly from a loudspeaker I usually use the surfaces of the environment itself as the sources of sound.

The most interesting acoustic shapes in the Bell Gallery were the corners. There were many; room dividers formed twelve extra corners in the space (Illustration 1). By pointing speakers from the ceiling (at an angel where they couldn't be heard directly) into each, the corners themselves, with their complex patterns of reflection and acoustic shadows, became the perceived sources of sound. Six synthesizers were connected to different groupings of the sixteen sources so that each synthesizer formed a three dimensional shape composed of two or three corners in the space.

I have always used electronics to generate the sounds of my installations. It is simply the best "paint" we have for sound today. The arguments about "acoustic" as opposed to electronic sound sources seem false to me. Sound is not like wood, -- we can have real wood and synthetic wood. Sound is sound and unless one bypasses the ears (perhaps an intriguing idea) a sound generated electronically is just as real as a sound made by a violin. Violins and pianos don't grow on trees, but are in fact rather antique "synthesizers" from the mechanical age.

I think the distinction between acoustic and electronic was made originally because of the primitive nature of early electronic sound sources, something which is no longer true. It continues today as an argument about control between the technician and the musician. To use the term electronic music as a means of classification becomes meaningless when we realize that all recorded music has become electronic music by the act of recording it.

For me, the transition of moving from using "acoustic" sound sources to electronic ones was a gradual one. It began while I was still

236

# Illustration 1

The sound sources were invisible and complex. Sixteen speakers, placed near the ceiling and disguised as light fixtures, were pointed at the sixteen corners of the space. This caused the corners themselves, with their complex patterns of reflection and acoustic shadows, to become apparent sources of sound. The speakers were combined into six sound channels. These channels were made up of two or three speakers in different locations. Each channel formed a sound source shape within the room.

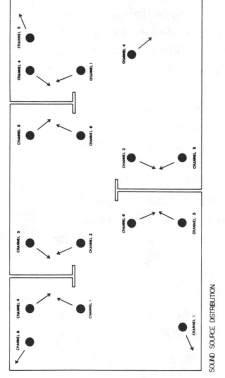

SOUND SOURCE DISTRIBUTION

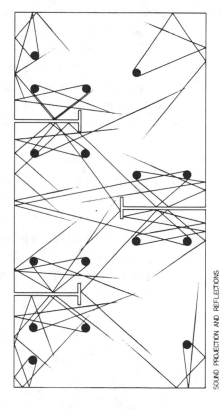

SOUND PROJECTION AND REFLECTIONS

NEUHAUS, SOUND INSTALLATION
BELL GALLERY
LIST ART CENTER
BROWN UNIVERSITY
PROVIDENCE, RHODE ISLAND
FEBRUARY - MARCH, 1983

DRAWING 1

237

working as a percussionist. Knowing nothing about electronics, I became intrigued with possibilities of extending the tone color of the traditional instruments I was working with. At that time there were few electronic sound making or processing devices available, so I began teaching myself about electronic circuits which could make and change sounds.

For *Fan Music* (1968) I built eight electro-mechanical solar sound sources. Ventilating fans placed between photocells and the sun generated a sound waveform which changed in tone color as the sun moved across the sky, an disappeared as it set. The work was made for an urban terrain, the multi-leveled rooftops of four adjoining buildings in Manhattan. The eight sources were dispersed on different levels to form and aural topography to match the physical one (Illustration 2).

I was interested in working with groups of independent sound sources. Ideas about stereo and quadrophonic sound seemed to have more to do with recreation than creation. The real sound world is, in fact, formed by a multitude of sound sources each one contributing a small part of the whole. For me, space is as important a sound dimension as the sound itself. During the years up until 1979, I built a special set of sound sources for each work. The most complex of these being the permanent work in the museum of contemporary art in chicago, with thirty sound sources (Illustration 3).

As my work became concerned with larger groups of sources, I became interested in computers as a means to control arrays of sound synthesizers -- using the computer to edit, store, retrieve and compare sound structures for many independent sound sources. Many applications of computers use the machine for analysis, simulation and modeling, utilizing their facility and flexibility as a means of design and planning for a future physical reality. By using a computer to generate sound, though, one is at the same time *also* able to create that physical reality, a very great advantage for that reality is as malleable as a model.

The early days of making sound works with computers were plagued with many difficulties, the major one being the inability to

Illustration 2

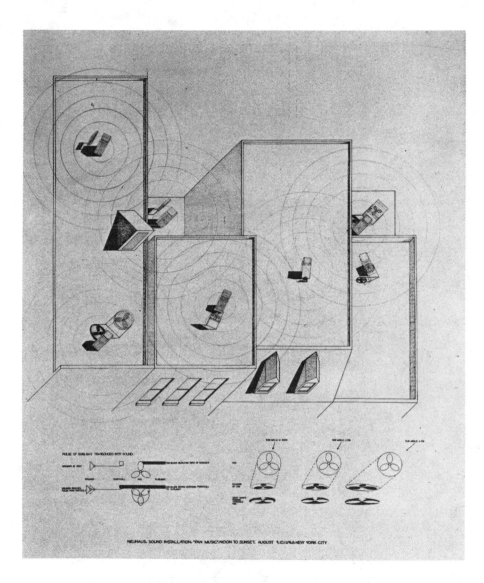

Illustration 3

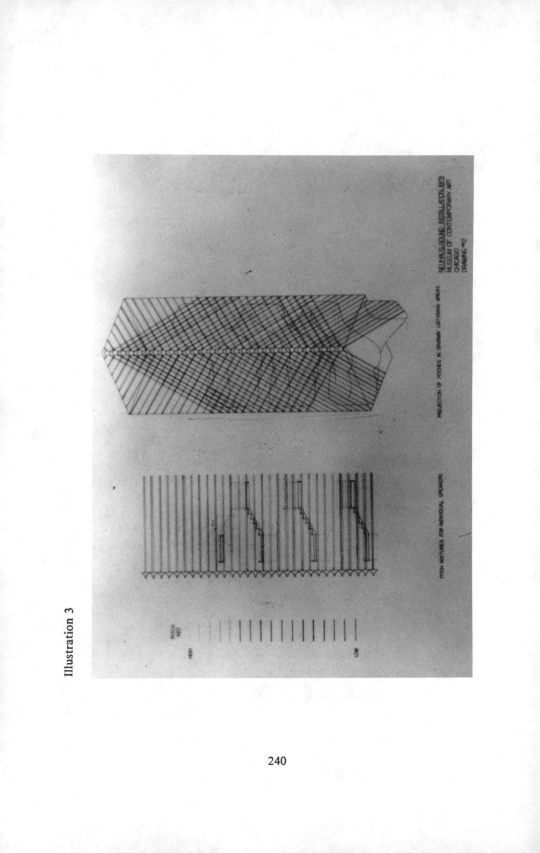

240

hear what you were doing. The machine took so long to calculate the sound that in many institutions the combination of computing time and bureaucracy meant that it took a week after you had made something before you could hear it.

The most powerful means we have of directing the creation of sound is the ear in conjunction with the human mind. To try to make a work without hearing is analogous to trying to drive a car without seeing. The current state of technology still can't measure things which the ear can hear and the science of psychoacoustics has only begun to sketch the outlines of what sound means to us. Nevertheless, this inability to hear what one was doing seems to have spawned several generations of composers who negated the ear in favor of the rather limited, albeit precise, description of reality provided by science and the language of mathematics. The current crop of sound synthesizers has moved the ability to use computers to work with sound, out of the institution and into the hands of individual composers. Because these machines are designed specifically to make sound one can quite easily hear what one is doing.

The work at Brown used the first version of a computer controlled sound synthesizer array which I built to use as a basic tool for not one work, but many. The system, first used for the work in the botanical garden in St. Paul in 1980, consisted of sixty-four independent synthesizers under the control of a microcomputer. The computer allowed sets of synthesizer parameter values to be chosen and patterns of these values which varied in time to be created and stored for each synthesizer.

As I work within the space itself, the problem of hearing what I am doing has another dimension. It becomes hearing what I am doing, *where* I am doing it, hence I have a need for a system which I can operate by remote control. Something which allows me to make sounds and structures -- changing and comparing them from any point in the installation site. In this preliminary version of the system I used a long cable connected to a battery operated TV monitor and a light pen.

At the present time, (1986) the array I am using is a network of sound synthesis computers. It extends the original concept by making each source an independent computer with up to 100 simultaneous tasks. Rather than a central computer controlling individual synthesizers the central computer is used to program the individual computers, which control the synthesizers. The remote control unit is now wireless and has a range of a half mile for large scale installations.

For the work in the Bell Gallery I used a subset of the early system. After fixing the corners of the space as sources of sound I spent a day exploring their character and the character of the room itself with different kinds of sound. Moving around the space, making sounds and listening from various points. Building up a library of sounds and getting a feeling for how they worked in the space. The following morning I decided to use a series of short clicks -- quasi-pitched sounds like finger snapping which I could vary in tone color.

Many of my sound installations are stable aural topographies which listeners explore and interpret individually by moving through them. Others are made with moving sound images. The first of these was *Walk Through* (1973) which was also the first unmarked work in a public place (Illustration 4). The moving image was one way of providing an "entrance" to the work. The initial listener impression of a moving sound image is that something is in fact moving near by. While seeking visual conformation one begins to listen.

In *Walk Through* the sound movement was controlled by weather conditions, an idea I was working with at the time of connecting the work to its environment so that it became an evolving process. A casual way of subtly changing it so that it was never the same. I abandoned this way of working when I found that it was preventing people from finding the work -- many thought of the work as some kind of new weather gimmick.

At Brown I was interested in creating a strong sound image which would seem to move around the space sort of like aural lightning flashes, but very subtle and soft -- just barely perceptible.

I decided to make a five click phrase and move it through overlapping channels. The click phrase was a little less than a second long consisted of five fast pulses followed by an equal period silence. Each phrase was composed of linked

Illustration 4

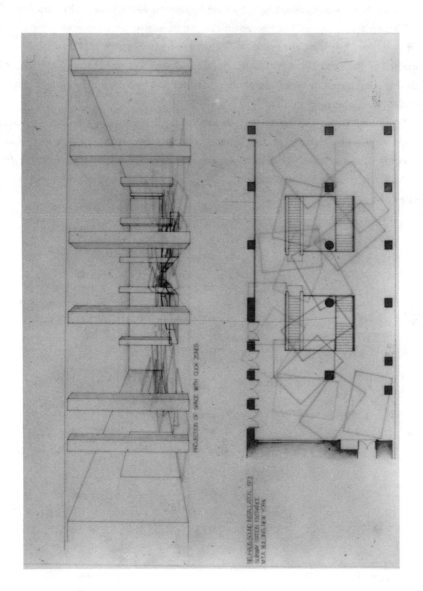

pulse pairs. The first click of a phrase appeared in one channel shape. The second click was actually composed of two simultaneous clicks -- a click from the new channel shape along with the repetition of the first channel. The third click was a third channel shape and a repeat of the second channel, and so forth (Illustration 5).

This structure linked the perception of the pulses into a phrase which seemed to pivot as it moved around the room. -- Each new phrase with a different pathway. Independent of the evolution of these click phrase pathways was second evolution of click timbre -- the tone color of the changed from light to dark and back again at an independent speed in each channel.

Sound installations of mine use sound to actualize imaginary places -- places to explore aurally or simply to be in. The sound is not the work, the place is -- the sound is only the catalyst which creates the sense of place. The listener entering the Bell Gallery was confronted with an empty space -- he began to find his place when he noticed the sound.

# Illustration 5

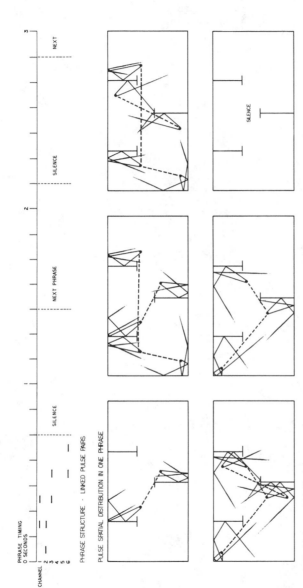

PHRASE TIMING
0 SECONDS

CHANNEL
2
3
4
5
6

PHRASE STRUCTURE - LINKED PULSE PAIRS

PULSE SPATIAL DISTRIBUTION IN ONE PHRASE

SILENCE

NEXT PHRASE

SILENCE

NEXT

2

3

SILENCE

SILENCE

The click phrase consisted of five fast
pulses within a three quarter second
period, followed by an equal period of
silence. Each phrase was composed of
linked pulse pairs. The first click of a
phrase appeared in one channel configuration. The second click was actually
composed of two simultaneous clicks — a
click from a new channel configuration
along with the repetition of the first
channel. The third click was a third
channel configuration with the repeat of
the second click channel, and so forth.
This structure linked the pulses into a
phrase which seemed to pivot as it moved
around the room.

NEUHAUS, SOUND INSTALLATION
BELL GALLERY
LIST ART CENTER
BROWN UNIVERSITY
PROVIDENCE, RHODE ISLAND
FEBRUARY - MARCH 1983

DRAWING 2

245

Words and Spaces

David Dunn

DAVID DUNN was born in San Diego, California in 1953. He is an experimental composer and interdisciplinary theorist. He studied with composers David Ernst, Norman Lowrey and Kenneth Gaburo. As an assistant to Harry Partch, he was active as a performer of Partch's music and is considered an expert on this composers unique musical theories and instruments. His music and writings have appeared in a variety of international forums, concerts, broadcasts, exhibitions and publications. He has received grants and commissions from the San Diego Ballet Co., The National Endowment for the Arts, The University of New Mexico (Albuquerque, New Mexico), Drew University (Madison, New Jersey), The National Gallery of Victoria (Melbourne, Australia), and Meet the Composer (New York, New York). In addition, he is the author of several books including *Skydrift* (Lingua Press, 1979) and *Music, Language, and Environment* (Atopia Press, 1988).

One of David Dunn's primary interests has been the exploration of the interrelationships between a variety of geophysical phenomena, environmental sound and music. These include: the unusual resonance characteristics of specific geographies; intensification of environmental sensing; the linguistic analysis of environmental ambience patterning; and the interactive application of technology in ways which make problematic any comfortable assumptions about the relationship of technology to nature.

David Dunn has taught at San Diego State University, Southwestern College in Chula Vista, California and Drew University in Madison, New Jersey. He is currently President of the International Synergy Institute in Santa Fe, New Mexico.

# An Expository Journal of Extractions From Wilderness

## notes toward an environmental language

### David Dunn

1.

Is my primary responsibility as a composer merely the creation of substantive concepts and structures, or am I responsible for the formation and maintenance of a proper environment for such structures?

Beyond this the question must be asked:

*What are the contextual limits for such an environment and of what might appropriate maintenance consist?*

I assert that the significance of this question is particularly relevant to discussions addressing the *musical acquisition of technology* at a time when the sheer immensity of technological resources constrains the survival of living systems in such a way that I must confront the *technological acquisition of music.*

Despite what may be seen as obvious predispositions intrinsic to certain technologies, rendering their function more readily exploitable by industrial and political power structures, it remains a commonly held belief that the user has autonomous responsibility to determine if the signals generated from use of a particular tool are input to or output from a given social context.

*But to what extent do I have free choice in either selection of my tools or in what I make with them?*

The culture of technology asserts its values with relentless force. It constrains behavior in convention with such values while maintaining the facade of its neutrality. Machines are not neutral objects, they are vestiges of thought empowered with the force of intent.

Thus, the issue of what is appropriate maintenance begins to occupy a larger context, namely:

*the mere creation of structures is not sufficient if either the means for their making or the environment in which they must reside contribute to the negation of those structures.*

Additionally I must recognize that all technology is part of a larger structure: *the adaptive whorls of organic energy blossoming into living system;* and that the dialectic of exploitation surrounding the influence of technology must therefore include the whole of the biotic world.

2.

We reside in a fabric of communication,
the environment's language encoded in the patterns of its living systems.
As our species moves forward with the purposeful extinction
of others forms of life at the current rate of one species per day,
it appears that how we converse with this fabric
has much to with the continuation of life on this planet.

Whatever understanding we may have of our place among these systems, it must be directed toward the hope that this earth has spawned us for some other purpose than its own destruction.

3.

Energy from the sun to the earth seems destined to cause an increasingly ordered state in the organization of matter. The compounding of structures of matter into more complex organizations which cannot be described in terms of their simpler components, stops at the level of simple molecules. Living organisms, however, continue this buildup integrating more complex patterns of organization such that molecules become macromolecules, then organelles and finally cells. The rather mysterious processes of evolution continue with the combining of cells into higher organisms. Various terms have been proposed to describe this phenomenon such as *negentropy or syntropy*, but what they fundamentally refer to is this innate drive in living organisms toward interaction, growth, and complexity. The *Gaia Hypothesis*, proposed by James Lovelock, theorizes that the biosphere has strategically programmed its evolution for three billion years. The extraordinary implication is that the whole of the biosphere is akin to one incredibly large living organism. Support for such a contention is based upon observations about the Earth's extremely unlikely atmospheric makeup, suggesting that the composition of the atmosphere is itself a biological construction resulting as a consequence of an immense cybernetic system termed Gaia which seeks optimal conditions for the totality of planetary life.1 Inherent in the interaction of these systems is the exchange and transformation of communication energy. More precisely this could be termed the transmission of *difference*. The inevitable complex increase in condensation of this energy within societies of higher organisms generates language. What seems evident about the extreme compression of these energies in human languages is that the various realities in which we are engaged are themselves shaped and constrained by language constructs. The mental world does not stop at the boundaries of the flesh, nor is it inside my head. Mind is a compound phenomenon of interacting parts bounded arbitrarily by what I either wish to or am capable of understanding. In other words, mind consists of organism in and of environment. Although I recognize my subjectivity to be inescapable, I am willing to contend that the dimensions of *self* actually consist of a vast interlocking network of eco-mental systems. How much of these larger systems are incorporated into self is a function of my language, determining at what point I limit connection with what appears to be the outer world. If I reduce the dimensions of self to extreme exiguity, I subsequently decrease the interaction with those systems necessary to sustain life.

4.

The act of description is not passive, I speak in the place of what is described and in one sense become its representative. Responsible representation demands accuracy gained through interaction: *listening as expansion of connection within the biotic world*. It is not trivial to assert that when humanity ceases to listen to the voice of wolf or whale, hindering their survival, we help to limit the biosphere's potential reality toward our own destructive short term advantage.

Biologist Gregory Bateson has stated:
> There is an ecology of bad ideas, just as there is an ecology of weeds, and it is characteristic of the system that basic error propagates itself. It branches out like a rooted parasite through the tissues of life, and everything gets into a rather peculiar mess.2

The making of creative connections between phenomena involves the disassembling of reality constructs with which I operate in blind assumption. I consist of more than I recognize. Freedom is not just having choice among a set of contrived possibilities, it is fundamentally the expanding of what I do not know, expanding the connection with what I previously thought outside myself. Most current socio-economic systems reward attempts to make social and biotic systems predictable. Predictability is achieved through redundancy introduced as subsequent loss of choice. High predictability yields low information and therefore less freedom. For example, the diversity of the food we currently eat diminishes almost daily. Large corporate takeovers of the patented seed industry has recently put pressure on world governments to centralize the manufacture of seeds in order to guarantee industry profit. Laws have been passed in both the United States and Europe which outlaw certain unpatented plants. The European *Common Catalog* lists all varieties which remain legal to grow, and over a year's time literally hundreds of plants are removed from the list. Stiff fines are levied against gardeners who attempt to grow these illegal varieties. It has been estimated that these attempts to ensure corporate profits will result in three-quarters of all European vegetable varieties becoming extinct by 1991.[3]

5.
Human consciousness of nature is itself an event in nature which contributes to its transformation. As consciousness, in the form of culture, folds back upon the biosphere pushing toward civilization, the energy absorbed from the surrounding environment, necessary to sustain the decrease of internal entropy within consciousness, is subsequently excreted not only as waste but as disruption of the surrounding organic systems. This would seemingly result in a consumption of energy exceeding what the environment is capable of sustaining. In other words, there is probably an essential point of equilibrium between the growth rate of civilization and the capability of supporting life systems to supply energy, beyond which breakdown of the total system begins. For example, the *1978 Conservation Biology Conference* predicted the probable end of vertebrate evolution by the turn of the century, including massive extinction of many species.[4] Perhaps the point beyond where equilibrium is maintained is also the point at which redundancy sets in: culture becomes positive feedback generating more waste than knowledge.

Technology is a *culture* which by its overwhelming power either absorbs or eradicates biological, cultural, and linguistic diversity. In view of this, it seems trivial to ask what effect technology has had upon music instead of asking, what of music might remain unaffected? To find such a phenomenon is probably also to absorb it since as a member of such a culture I begin to hear with technological ears. The very choice of whether to use or not use technology to disseminate my ideas has largely been taken away from me. Thus the question remains: do my ideas attempt to disintermediate this cultural redundancy or merely reinforce it? By now it must seem obvious that the naive fascination with new machines is not only trivial but dangerous. The well-worn assertion that technology is neutral, awaiting specific use by good or evil people, is a cliche whose idiocy is only compounded by equating advances in music with advances in machines. It places music in a status similar to mineral resources where values await the strip-mining mentality of commercialization. International industrialization and the energy consumption which feeds it have unfortunately become synonymous with social evolution. Discussions about technology inevitably link it to notions of progress which demand consumptive and centralized economies. Machines are somehow thought to signify the future while skills derived from living interactively with the biotic environment are thought to represent the past. Technology is not merely the manufacture and use of tools: it is a residue of how we imagine the world into being. It is an environment of symbols against whose institutions we must each day pit our needs or conform to that environment's mechanization. Beyond the residue of our imaginings is the freedom of the yet unknown. At best technology is merely the collective debris upon which we may stand in further imagining; at worst, technology is the refuse within which to bury choice.

6.
Near where I live is a coastal estuary set aside as a bird refuge.
This estuary lies north of a small group of hills and canyons
covered in the indigenous chapparal
(Southern California coastal scrub).
But surrounding this patch of uninhabited terrain
is the suburban sprawl of Southern California:

condominiums to the east;
private homes to the south;
and Interstate Highway 5 to the west,
with the Pacific Ocean just beyond.

Standing on these hills alone at night,
no matter is what direction turn,
I see lights flashing:

automobile headlights,
advertising searchlights,
airplanes,
streetlights,
and the eerie glow of television sets in windows.

Close to my feet are living things,
their presence illuminated by these abrupt and disparate bursts of lights.
Everything that struggles for life here must listen continuously,
all day and all night,
to the roar of nearby traffic.
It is beyond my imagination to believe
that what lives here is not changed by all of this;
or not changed by the web of communication network
which surrounds and entangles the biosphere.

It is an interesting activity to try and listen
to what this place has to tell me,
because for all my effort I cannot hear it;
the din of humanity is too loud.
It is a lonely thought that this disconnectedness
has been chosen by us.
Of what shall humanity consist when all that is left to hear
are the sounds of our isolation?

7.
My composition entitled *MADRIGAL: (The Language of the Environment is Encoded in Patterns of Its Living Systems)* began with a reticular notion: Perhaps each

254

instance of environmental ambience which I perceive is part of a much larger structure, that within the patterns of communication between living organisms there is a larger communication logic which each separate utterance combines with to form an environmental language. To decode a moment of this pattern might generate an appropriate language not only descriptive of a specific place and time, but more precisely a language descriptive of the mentality implicit in this connective instance: a composition *of* this environment and not merely *about* it.

The compositional process for *MADRIGAL* entailed the phonetic transcription of an environmental ambience recording made in the Cuyamaca Mountains of Southern California. One minute of recorded ambience provided the entire source material for the notated score. The transcription procedure involved attempting to bring the ambience into my physiology through both aural sensing and vocal emulation. Compositional organization of this transcription was made according to structural relationships intrinsic to the material itself.

In one sense *MADRIGAL* juxtaposes a primitive function of language (namely, to interact with the external environment) with one of the most recent analytical notations for language. Additionally my intention has been to combine multiple descriptions of a particular environment in order to convey: (1) a resonant sense of the richness of information contained in one spatial and temporal location; and (2) to exemplify the notion that most definitions of wilderness are not based upon interaction but are generalized abstractions which may or may not apply to a particular place.

1.  James E. Lovelock, GAIA, A new look at life on Earth  (Oxford University Press, 1979).

2.  Gregory Bateson, Steps to an Ecology of Mind (New York, Ballantine, 1972), p. 484.

3.  See Cary Fowler, "Sowing the Seeds of Destruction," in Science for the People (Sept./Oct., 1980), p.8.

4.  Science News, vol. 114, no. 13 (Sept. 23, 1978), p. 215.

This paper was first presented on August 26, 1981, at the International Music and Technology Conference, University of Melbourne, Victoria, Australia.

# MADRIGAL: (The Language of the Environment Is Encoded In the Patterns of Its Living Systems)

*David Dunn*

1980

# Performance Notes

*MADRIGAL* requires seven vocalist/reciters and a two-channel audio tape. The score is notated in the International Phonetic Alphabet (American Dialect of English) with additional signs. Articulation should emphasize the phonemes as if reciting them, the additional signs as timbral coloration only. Each numbered page is thirty seconds in duration with all individual lines temporally notated in spatial proportion to the page length. The tape playback amplitude should match the relative loudness of the live voices; no amplification of the voices should occur under any circumstances. Total duration of the composition is six minutes.

## NOTATION:

**vowels** (as in)

[i] beat
[I] bit
[ɛ] bet
[æ] bat
[a] ask
[ɑ] calm
[o] boat
[U] fool
[U] full
[ʌ] above
[ɜ] word

**consonants** (as in)

[m] sum
[n] sun
[p] pole
[b] bowl
[t] toll
[d] dole
[k] cool
[g] goal
[r] rot
[l] lot
[f] fat
[s] seal
[ð] thy
[ʃ] ash
[ʒ] azure
[h] hot
[w] watt

**combinations** (as in)

[ei] bait/beat
[hw] what

**other signs**

⊕ ingressive
◇ egressive
◉ hands cupped over mouth
• staccato
} whistle
↑
≺ throat rasp
pitch range
5 4 3 2 1
1—low to 5—high
~ trill
→ sustain

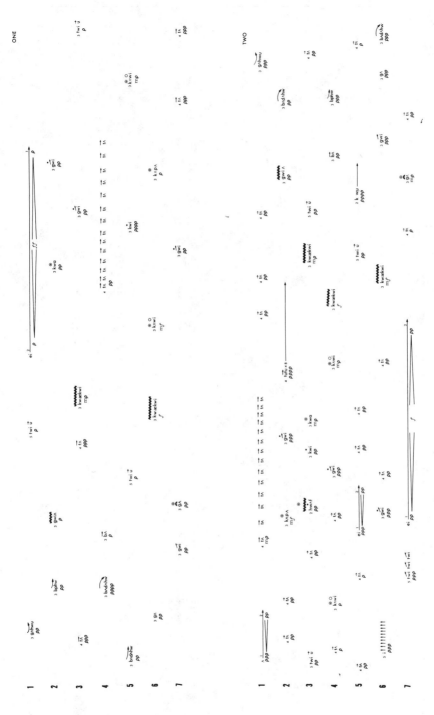

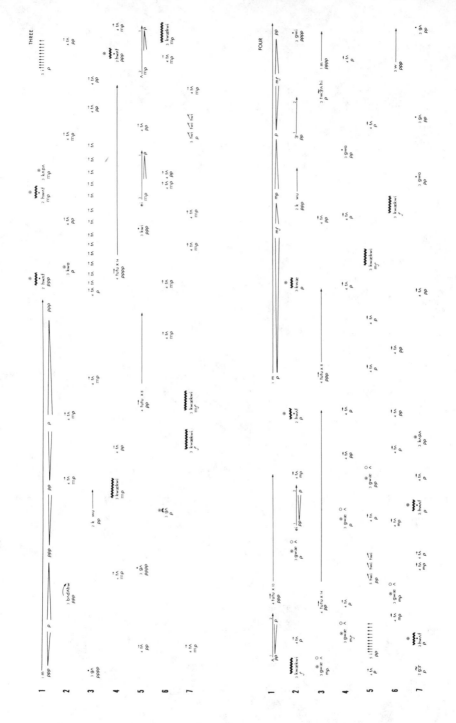

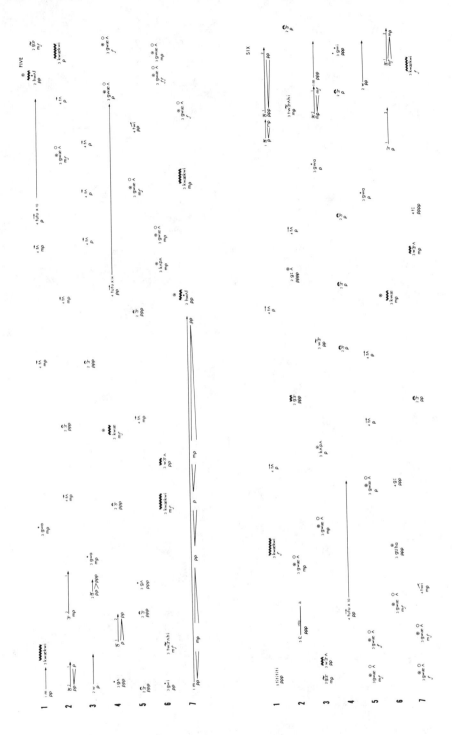

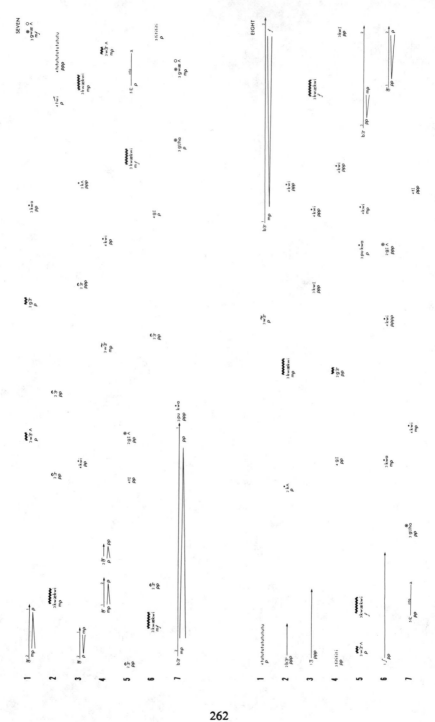

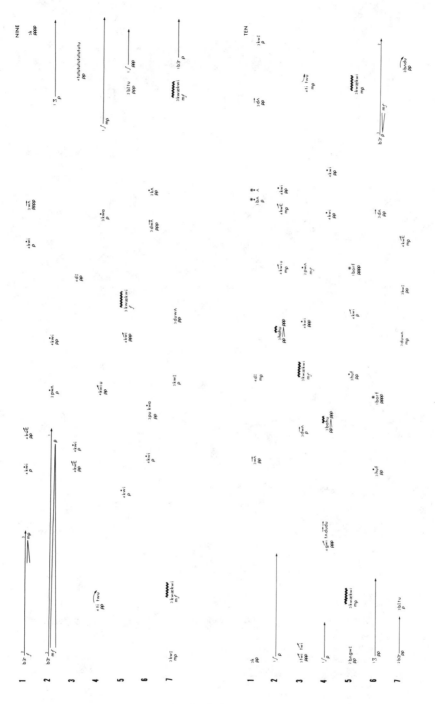

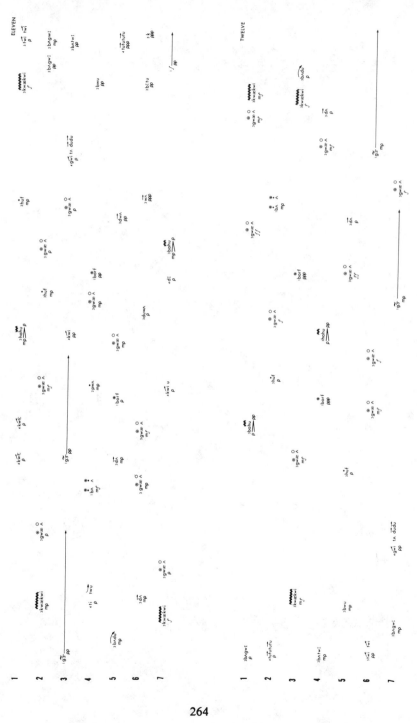